One For Sorrow, Two For Joy

ANGELA MERLANO

TABLE OF CONTENTS

INTRODUCTION

Tragedy is a path many people recognize but often refuse to acknowledge. So what do you do when the unthinkable happens? The brain goes into a panic mode, and we begin to reach for logic and reason. What happened to me made me reach for logic and reason, too.

On Tuesday, May 7, 2019, at my high school, STEM School Highlands Ranch, I was stuck in a lockdown for two hours, trapped during a shooting. My experience was one of a kind, one that I shared with two other high school peers and about thirty elementary kids.

What happened to me was undoubtedly unfair, but necessary. Often, when I saw posts on social media related to mass shootings, I pitied the victims and the community, never realizing it's something that affects you forever. When the tables turned, and the news of my school was posted about, I didn't feel pity any longer—I felt sympathy. I no longer saw victims; I saw survivors. My perspective changed for the better.

I had a community I could rely on. Yet, I still felt alone due to the fact that I bottled up my emotions. I hope that by sharing my journey, I can accomplish the following: be there for others, change perspectives, and inform others.

I wish to reach out to any survivors of mass shootings, no matter how big or small. Communities form from these tragedies, and I hope that writing a book about this experience can help other survivors. It's hard knowing what to do when everyone around you is figuring it out at the same time. I, for one, experienced a lot of uncertainty. I disliked my emotions at the beginning—then, I learned that it's better to feel things out, even if it's uncomfortable.

I also want to change perspectives. It's easy to be ignorant on these topics and assume that things would have gone differently if something else was tried—maybe if exhibited behavior was seen earlier, Alec and Devon could've sought counsel. However, whether you're a survivor or not, you can't blame anything or anyone else for a shooting, except the one who had the gun. It took me time to acknowledge that these tragedies are unpredictable and can happen regardless of effort to stop it beforehand. You can't blame yourself or the innocent people around you for the difficult things that happen. I learned that the hard way. After all, how can things begin to change for the future, if we always dwell on the past?

Lastly, I want to inform others of my experience. I want to let others know that being a survivor isn't easy, and pity from others makes it harder. Often, in my experience, people outside of the STEM community would tell lengthy condolences or pity me, especially if they're new to the situation. It felt cheap and half-baked to me. I hope this book, this experience, can teach others the right way to encounter survivors like me.

Please note, I have no intention of harming the school or any survivors of the shooting. I want to share my unique experience that I had as a student during and after the incident. I hope this touches somebody's heart, and I hope this book can be a wakeup call to ignorant minds and closed hearts.

I also have no intention of glorifying or crediting any mass shooters or school shooters. They deserve no praise and have caused horrible pain to families, children, and even their own peers.

I'd like to acknowledge my friends, my family, and every single person changed because of a school shooting.

I'd also like to acknowledge the Castillo family—John, Maria, and Kendrick. Without Kendrick's sacrifice joined by the bravery of a few others, I wouldn't be writing this now. Kendrick was brave enough to face danger—he will always be a hero to me. He deserves recognition for his sacrifice. Kendrick is truly a saint.

John and Maria have experienced an inexplicable loss, yet are still giving and generous to the community. They deserve the absolute best, and I am forever grateful to both of them for giving me the courage and the heart to heal. My family instantly connected with them, and I am thankful for their openness and love. They are the foundation of the STEM community. Without them, I wouldn't have the inspiration to write this.

As a disclaimer, I'd like to add that some of the people included in my story expressed to me that they would prefer to stay anonymous. To accommodate their wishes, I use neutral terms or nameless descriptions.

Thank you. I hope you enjoy the book.

CHAPTER 1

One for sorrow, two for joy

Three for a girl, four for a boy

Five for silver, six for gold

Seven for a secret never to be told

Eight for a wish, nine for a kiss

Ten for something you must not miss

Eleven for health, twelve for wealth

Thirteen beware, it's the devil himself

This simple poem correlates to fate. On seeing magpies with iridescent feathers and a long tail, you count the birds and see what the fates hold in store for you. In the days leading up to the shooting, I saw single magpies often, and I wondered what it meant. Some would call me superstitious because I would count the birds every time I saw them, but I knew it was for a reason.

Tuesday, May 7, 2019—it's easy to recall the calm before the storm. It was a solemn day in the weather—rain clouds blanketed the sky, and for the first time, I heard rain pattering gently against the window of my math classroom.

The halls felt jittery, but strangely drained. Finals were hitting the upperclassmen hard. Freshmen, like me, were anticipating the summer. Back then it was easy. I didn't feel as if I had to take anything seriously. I had just got into a relationship with this boy I was crushing on for a while—Charlie. I was already planning for things we'd do over the summer. I got up to stand next to my classmates who were staring outside at the rain. Class was about to begin and I was bored of sitting idly at my desk. Plus, chilly rain in May was a sight to behold. I usually walked to the cafe that was up the street, but I was thinking of just asking Charlie to drive me there. We could meet up with our friends, hang out, and talk, just like we did every day. It's almost pitiful how I had such innocent plans and suggestions in my head before it happened.

The math period ended, and I prepared to head to my final class of the day—music production. It was my favorite class, especially since I met Charlie there. I walked inside and scanned the chairs splayed about for students, hoping to spot Charlie and sit next to him. To my surprise, I didn't see him there.

I waited a few minutes after the bell before asking our teacher about it. He told me to sit down and wait since he would explain soon anyway. Our class was divided up into middle schoolers and upperclassmen, so I sat with the other two classmates my age, as usual, and waited.

Our teacher soon explained that Charlie was away due to an AP test, and said that it would cause a change of plans. I suddenly remembered about the project we had to do that day—we had to record elementary students for an end-of-the-year talent show.

Charlie was going to pair up with me to go to one classroom upstairs, and the other two would stay in the homeroom to record and configure audio there. With Charlie gone, I had to go with the others instead. I was unenthused—I wasn't great at configuring technology, so I wouldn't do much, especially with Charlie gone. He would invite me to try figuring things out myself, but these two would just want the job done.

We packed up and got ready to move to the elementary section. After a short dilemma, I decided to leave my backpack in the music room. I didn't think I would need my laptop anyway.

I saw my friend enter the middle school English room as we walked past to get to the stairwell to the elementary. STEM is divided into three parts: the elementary, middle school, and high school. Classrooms could share between each section.

As I passed by my friend, I waved to him and shared a gesture that we used every time we saw each other—similar to the "rock on" hand signal. He was entering the English classroom in the middle school area. He seemed shaken, so I asked if he was okay, and he told me he was fine. He was holding a black backpack, sort of in a strange way, as it was bulging. I thought nothing of it and continued to the elementary.

My peers and I prepared to record the kids showing off their talents. Then we began to record a girl playing piano. I didn't do much to help. I waited for further instruction and kept my arms crossed. A lot was on my mind. I had to write a comedy play for a project, finish a music assignment, study for a few tests, and more.

I looked outside the large windows and saw a blonde teacher run outside. A handful of young students joined her. I thought it was peculiar.

I heard "middle school lockdown" from the public address system. Soon after, they announced a general lockdown. "Attention please: lockdown. Lock, lights, out of sight" was the phrase that was repeated. We turned off the lights and went to sit against the wall that was next to the door. I wondered if it was an insignificant problem—a coyote or wild animal entering the school. After all, this was Colorado. I became indifferent to the situation and went on my phone. The teacher looked at me and tapped my shoulder. He asked me to get off of my phone in a polite tone, describing that the potential threat could find me through the light of my phone. I got annoyed but still turned it off.

My friend looked over at me and began to whisper, a jocular smile on his face.

"Oh, shit, it's finally happening. Do you think it's a school shooter?"

Panic shot through my body. Yet, I remained calm and began to joke along. "Oh, crap, we left our backpacks downstairs in the music room and my lip balm is there!"

"Can't die without your lips moisturized."

We chuckled, our voices barely above a whisper, but my panic and anxiety returned as if it never left. My hands got cold at the fingertips and began to tremble. My legs and arms had shivers running through them.

Forty minutes passed by, and the teacher asked me and my friends to hide behind a desk next to the white board. It was a brown circular desk. It didn't provide much cover, but it was still the least they could do. The two teachers began to pace, then sit down, then check the windows. I could see police lights and ambulances when I lifted my head to peek. This was taking too long for a small threat, like a wild animal. We would have been outside by now if that were the case. I began assuming the worst.

Texts were popping up on my phone. Me, my brother Luke, and my dad were in the conversation on a family group chat.

My dad texted, *Lockdown confirmed in STEM area. What's going on?*

Luke and I were unsure. I wanted to depend on him for any information that was incoming, since he was on the first level of the school. Then, a few moments later, I received the scariest text I have ever read.

The words popped up near my text bar: *Confirmed school shooter.*

My hands began to shake again, this time in a more violent manner, and I started to look around. One of the children asked to have a trashcan to throw up out of anxiety. I was still unsure, so I decided to wait until I got real evidence.

I asked one of the teachers to read the texts I received. Concern grew on his face. He went over to his teacher aid, a bigger guy, and suggested the idea of blocking the doors.

We watched the teachers move two large stereo amplifiers to the two entryways. He looked at us, mouthing to us that it was there, just in case the threat came by. One of the amplifiers produced a large bang, and we all shrank away in fear that the noise gave our location away. After all, we heard no gunshots, a few shouts here and there—so we were unsure where the threat was. It might as well have been down the hall.

One of my peers asked me to turn down the volume on the audio interface as I was next to it, so that it wouldn't make noise.

With trembling hands, I moved down the knob and went back to the texts on my phone.

My older brother Jimmy had recently read the texts and replied, *What the hell?!* He suggested driving over to pick us up, due to the school trapping us. My dad advised against it, and my brother waited from a distance.

My friend then tapped my shoulder and showed me a post on his phone. I read over the post from the Douglas County Sheriff. I read it for the first time, only reading the words "confirmed shooter," "police," and "AMC." I gained instant relief, believing that the shooter was at the theater near our school.

I was wrong.

I asked him to show it to me again. I read it over several times. The shooter was in our school. My second home for years. They mentioned the theater in the post so that police could protect the area.

The whispers among the adults gave an immense anxiety to the children. I couldn't cry or seem afraid—the teacher asked me to "keep my cool" for the younger kids. I prayed to myself in silence and began to sing a church hymn in my head. I was unsure why I sang that song in specific, one that spoke of salvation after death. Perhaps it was because I was afraid I would die. My eyes watered, but I let no tears fall. The teachers asked me if I was okay and I assured them I was.

I remembered Charlie. I remembered that he had the AP test that day. If only he was there with me, then I wouldn't be so afraid. I texted him and asked him where he was, how he was, and if he was okay. I had no idea if they took away his phone before the test. As I kept overthinking, my intense worry only increased; I loved him.

My thoughts continued racing as I noticed my current surroundings. The children were whimpering and muttering words, collapsing into the arms of the teacher, Mr. Paul.

"What's happening?"

"I wanna see my mom."

"I don't wanna die."

The heart-wrenching phrases rivaled the powerful repetition from the P.A.

My friend began to dance in a subtle manner to the repeated phrase as a joke in an attempt to cheer me up. I smiled weakly for half a second, but I didn't have the strength to laugh.

I looked over at Mr. Paul, cradling the children and reassuring them. It must've taken so much bravery to keep it together for them.

We heard a loud bang in the distance. A collective whine from the unsure children rose.

I then heard maracas. My peers and I looked confused as we mouthed to each other, "maracas?" Luke texted that the same could be heard on the first level. We later figured out it was the sound of tasers in use.

It seemed like forever that we were waiting in that room, shivering and anxious. I saw my phone was almost dead, so I put it on low power mode. In that particular model of phone, it dimmed everything down, removed the wallpaper, and force stopped apps that weren't for communication or emergencies. It made the situation all the more real and all the more frightening. I was terrified of my phone dying. What if something happened to me, and I couldn't contact anybody about it? What if I wouldn't be able to contact my family?

We heard a loud banging on our door, and a projected masculine voice shouting, "Open the door!" Mr. Paul didn't hesitate to rise up, throw the amplifier away from the entrance, and then open the door. Someone in tan clothing and armed with a rifle of some sort shouted into the room. "Get the fuck out!"

Mr. Paul stepped aside as a few officers stormed into the room.

"Is everyone okay?" a female officer stepped in and surveyed the room.

We all nodded to the officer's question. They then ordered us to put our hands over our heads. I was carrying the orange Nalgene my boyfriend gave to me a few weeks ago.

We were all organized into a line so we could step out of the room and into safety.

Then the officer talked to my two friends and I. "Do you guys mind standing in the back? You're older and you could watch over these kids."

We nodded and organized ourselves at the back of the line. The officers led us out, and I remember letting tears fall down my face. The kids weren't depending on me to be brave anymore, and reality was setting in. I could finally cry. I wept as we walked out of the room and then down the stairs.

My friend, who was joking about lip balm earlier, asked me if I was okay.

"It's scary, it's fucking scary," I replied, smiling in disbelief.

As I stepped outside, one single magpie perched on the pole close to me. It screeched and flapped its wings. It was as if the universe was mocking me.

CHAPTER 2

We made it outside, where we were safe. I saw many kids evacuated on a field across the street. It was cold. I could feel the
wind on my face against my wet tears, and I felt so grateful to feel
the cold again. We were finally away from the repeated phrase, the
phrase that meant danger.

Officers were reassuring us, telling us we were okay and that
we were safe as we walked toward the field. I traced the crowd of
students with my eyes. I saw a few acquaintances and friends, but not
Charlie or Luke. Panic and anxiety instilled in me again. Yet, it was
a peculiar feeling, seeing everyone from my school on this field. I
spotted the girl I was envious of, crying in the arms of her friend; the
loud kid who annoyed everyone with howls in the hall, hugging his
knees and waiting silently; the quiet kid who was always in the back
of class, pacing and looking for her favorite teacher with panicked
eyes. I realized it didn't matter who we were or what we had—in that
moment, we were all in the same boat.

As I walked on the asphalt, people in my line began dispers-
ing and running to familiar faces. I glanced around hurriedly at the

crowd before me, filled with students who had concerned expressions on their faces as they looked for the people they knew. We all wanted to make sure our friends were alive. Luke was sending texts, but I was still unsure of his whereabouts, and I needed the comfort of my sibling. Charlie was my primary focus, especially due to his lack of communication. I was worried sick, sending text after text with a loss of hope. I looked at the bundles of students huddled together, hoping I'd be able to find him just by scrolling my eyes through the crowd. Then, out of nowhere, my eyes landed on him coming toward me. The first person I encountered happened to be Charlie. The moment I saw his face, I hurried over to him. He, as well, rushed immediately to greet me the minute he spotted me coming over.

I jumped into his arms. He hugged me tight, and I hugged him back. I sobbed and sobbed, hyperventilating and weeping into his shoulder as he held me. He rubbed my back, and whispered consolations into my ear. It was ironic that he had the strength to console me—but I wasn't surprised. That was the reason I loved him, the reason he was Charlie. I pulled away to kiss him, seeing that he had been crying as well. His eyes were watery and tinted red.

"I was so scared you were dead or something!" I wailed to him. Charlie reassured me repeatedly, told me he was there, and hugged me again.

The next person I saw was Luke and his partner—also a close friend of mine. I was so thankful, I cried upon seeing the two. We were bundled into a tight hug, and I wept again into Luke's shoulder.

My other friends rushed up to me and hugged me as well. My friend Sebastian told me that Charlie was so anxious looking for me, wondering if I was safe. It comforted me that he worried as well.

We all waited there for a while, seeing what was next. The grass was rough; the gray sky made the atmosphere cold and rigid. I stood among my peers—some were hunched over crying, some were sobbing into friends' arms, and others looked around with wide and anxious eyes, as if concerned that the threat was among us. I asked questions—asked who the shooter was, where they were, and where my other friends were.

I found out that some of my friends evacuated to the other side of the school, which relieved me immensely. I texted them and wondered if they were okay.

I then finally heard numbers. Around seven or eight were injured, and there was one casualty. I wondered who the eight were and if they were okay. People began talking about a third shooter on the run, and I got anxious that they were close by, waiting for the right moment to light us up. Later, we figured out that the third "shooter" was most likely our private security guard. He carried a concealed firearm against school policy and took it out when police entered the school. He shot as a reflex when he saw the barrel of an officer's gun around the corner. Still, I kept my wits about me and tried to stay close to Charlie. I never wanted to be apart from him again.

Charlie began to occupy me with some simple distracting games, like finger fencing and call-and-response campfire songs. It may have just been a tactic to calm me down and distract me, but it worked.

He grabbed my shoulders at one point. He told me, "Hey, if you're ever faced with a shooter, pretend you're dead until he leaves."

I nodded, but I was still smiling from our games.

"I'm serious, do you understand?"

I told him I did understand. He told me he loved me and that he would never let me be in danger again.

After what seemed like forever, they got us all into groups. Charlie and I were grouped with a handful of middle schoolers. We would be boarded onto buses so we could be transferred to a safer area later on.

It was cloudy and cold, and I desperately needed to pee. I drank water from the thirty-two-ounce Nalgene out of anxiety and to hydrate myself. I asked if I could use the restroom, and they asked if I could hold it. That too was torture.

On top of that, thunder began booming over our heads, and it started to rain. The loud crack of lightning scared many students. Some speculated that the police were using snipers. By now, I calmed down, so I doubted that the threat was still imminent.

A business nearby offered to keep us inside until the rain stopped, or until the buses arrived. They accommodated us all inside the medium-sized building. The fit was tight, but we were warm. The best part: I could finally use the restroom!

After I did my business, I returned to Charlie and found him talking to one of my friends. We were all desperate to go home, as several hours had already passed. I texted my parents and informed them of how everyone was doing, before my phone died. We weren't doing fantastic, but we survived.

We finally started to walk out group by group to the buses, but because of the heavy rain, we ended up rushing across the street. I stepped in unavoidable puddles, and my feet got soaked through the soles of my shoes. I had no jacket to shield me from the rain. It was a minor discomfort compared to what I just had to experience—and at least I was safe.

We ended up waiting a few minutes to board the bus in the rain. My hair got drenched before we finally got to board.

I shuffled next to other students, unable to sit next to Charlie and squished next to two middle schoolers. As he was filed into the seat in the back, he waved to me with a worried expression. I was slightly panicked, being away from him, but at least we were finally getting out of the school grounds. The seat across from me had two more middle schoolers, most likely friends of the two beside me. We waited a while before actually driving off. Yet, the younger students kept talking in loud voices, assuming and joking—I estimated that they were most likely not told anything so they wouldn't stress out.

Still, they speculated from rumors. They spoke of rumors about kids knocking on classroom doors and joking that it was safe to go outside. They spoke of the injured and the one who was killed. Those who still had their phone working shared information from their phones. I listened in, in desperation of wanting to know more details—no major news providers wrote on the shooting or what happened yet. It was too localized, too hidden, and I quickly became frustrated. I wanted to know everything at that moment: who did it, when it started, why it happened. I needed logic and reason.

As I sat sandwiched between the two middle schoolers, I contemplated on an event that happened just recently. A few weeks before, a woman named Sol Pais came to Colorado. She came to mock the twentieth anniversary of the Columbine High School shooting in 1999. She purchased a gun to threaten schools throughout Colorado school districts. Every school was shut down for the day out of precaution during the ongoing investigation. She ended up committing suicide out of fear when she was found by the police. The next day, teachers and staff addressed what happened with the intention to comfort us, a grim foreshadowing for the weeks to come.

I never fully understood how or why someone could do something so evil. I was terrified that day, regardless of being home the entire time. I told Charlie and my other friends to stay put and not go anywhere, just in case. If only I knew what was about to happen to me, not so much time later.

The rain and chill surrounding the bus made it difficult to drive in. I couldn't see outside very well, but I saw familiar places as we drove by. Some middle schoolers were writing "I AM A SURVIVOR" backward on the fogged bus windows. They hoped their message would affect somebody, let somebody know of their struggle.

I froze there, thinking, thinking, and thinking, as I didn't have Charlie to comfort me with his reason. Who could it have been? Are one of the shooters boarded with us, waiting for us to gather in a mass so they can kill us? Where *were* we going?

I was so disturbed by the fact that it happened in my own school. I was unsure if I would come back next year or not. Things were so uncertain. I had so much faith in the school; I used to feel safe.

I thought about that situation and I kept thinking to myself: why did it have to happen at my school? Where did we go wrong? Why did it have to be me?

No information on the shooters released yet, nor on the injured or the one killed. It was all a waiting game—waiting for the next report, for more stories, for different points of view. And my patience was wearing thin.

The bus came to a stop outside of the local recreation center, which was just down the way from the school. We were all ordered to go inside the covered tennis courts, not knowing what would happen next. I reunited with Charlie for a brief minute, but they had to search us for weapons. Hence, we were separated. They then instructed us to go to sections divided by last name. I waited in the M section, joined by Luke. I looked around for others who I didn't see before. Time passed, and Luke ignored the instructions and went to join friends. I worried that we would get in trouble, but I followed suit soon after. I joined a few of my peers who were discussing the incident. I greeted them and hugged them, asking if they were okay before talking about the shooting again. The anxiety felt terrible, like shocking waves of cold mixed with electricity tracing up and down my body. I could barely talk without my jaw shivering incessantly. It was a struggle between realizing the severity of what I had gone through and patronizing my own emotion.

"Do you have any idea who it was?" I asked.

My friend replied, "I don't know, some people are saying it's Alec or Devon, but I know they were in the middle school area."

Then my other friend spoke, his voice chattering. "No, it was definitely Alec."

I felt my gut twist, shocked at this new information.

I pushed off the negative thoughts. I pursued the conversation further, turning to my friend. It couldn't have been Alec. "Wait, Alec as in Alec Mckinney?" I asked and they confirmed that it was the most popular suspicion. I couldn't believe it. I greeted him earlier before he entered that classroom. I was so shocked. I wondered what would've happened if I insisted on talking to him. Prior to learning this, I looked everywhere for Alec and kept worrying where he was.

It was uncertain at the moment—a mere rumor. We knew it would take up to a day or two to come out with names. Yet, I continued to overthink. Although the indoor tennis court was warm, my skin collected goosebumps, and I felt myself go pale. While my friends continued to talk, I shivered, and my throat went dry. Alec, once a friend to me, was now a total stranger. The Alec I knew would never do something like that. The worst part was that I didn't even notice anything was wrong. Alec greeted me as usual before the shooting. Even earlier in the week, we talked amiably with each other.

I knew I couldn't blame myself. I can't. I couldn't have known at that exact moment. I was only shocked.

I borrowed a friend's phone to contact my mom and ask her who would pick us up. I found out that my older brother would. I felt relieved that eventually I would find myself out of this mess of a day.

After a while, they organized us by grade. Parents were waiting in a separate room, waiting to receive their child and take them home. I sat among my classmates in single file lines. Pretty soon, they were calling kids by name to reunite with their parents or guardians. We were talking among ourselves in hushed voices, then pausing once we heard a name.

I remember my friends sitting next to me and ignoring another girl who knew Alec well. She confessed that Alec and Devon would sit in Devon's car for weeks, talking.

A few others blamed her for not knowing sooner. At the time, I got angry as well—but nobody could have known. Not even her.

Students were leaving, one to two at a time. As people left, I got worried I would be stuck there for another two, three, or four hours. I didn't hear my name, and the lines were thinning out.

Before they called my other friend's name, she was judging the system they had to release the kids. Parents had to sign a waiver to the school before getting an identification paper. The waiver held the parents accountable for sending their child to school so that they couldn't sue.

As she was complaining, they shouted her name out. She was so eager to go home, she got up, kicking me as she did, and walked away in a hurry. Then only a few students were with me.

Finally, a teacher shouted as she held a paper in her hand, "Angela? Angela Merlano?" I looked up and responded in an instant with a loud "here!"

I didn't hesitate to rise and join the teacher. She led me to the reunion gate. I saw countless parents and guardians were hugging their kids. Others were looking for them in a hurry, or clinging against the tall mesh wall that divided us. I saw my older brother, Jimmy, waving at me and shouting my name. Luke was already there with him. I rushed over with my identification paper in hand. A teacher was trying to stop me from crossing over, but Jimmy grabbed me and pulled me away. They still pursued us and asked for our identification. I gave him my paper and Jimmy showed his ID. I finally saw Charlie again, who I wanted to come home with, but was already with his father. I told him it would be simpler if he came over later and he agreed. I wished them both farewell and told Charlie to text me.

Pretty soon, we hustled out of the tennis courts and made our way to Jimmy's truck.

The Salvation Army came, bringing food stations that provided sandwiches, pizza, and cookies for free. Luke and I took pizza and a few pink sugar cookies. As the anxiety and adrenaline settled, I grew hungry. We ate the food and moved as fast as possible. Jimmy was walking at a fast pace, and it was hard to keep up—I assumed he was angry. The atmosphere was quiet and eerie as students walked back with their parents, marching in a solemn matter. The only audible noises were sniffles and police chatter next to passing traffic.

CHAPTER 3

A news station was trying to receive interviews as families walked by. Jimmy pushed them away before they could record us, but I couldn't stop thinking to myself how inhumane it was to force cameras upon shaken children. That week, I never hated the media more. I felt as though I was a statistic, a pawn in their political game. I refused to be, and so did many others.

We reached Jimmy's truck. It was sunny, but the dark clouds still covered the skies. It felt surreal, as if it was all a weird nightmare.

Jimmy told us that an angel of death passed the school that day. I could finally understand what came over the school.

The angel of death was watching me. He was watching me and everyone I knew, and somehow, that was the scariest part.

It was a quiet drive home. I wondered what my parents and my little brother went through. Oddly enough, I wondered if anybody texted me or asked if I was okay. At this point in time, my phone was dead, and all of the commotion halted me from finding a charger.

I reached home, and I saw my parents and my brother running out the door. He embraced me with a warm hug and I began to sob once more.

"I was so worried about you," I cried to my younger brother David.

I greeted my parents, and they hugged me tight. My mother told me she was so worried.

My dad suggested we step inside, as he felt being outside was unsafe at the moment. It was bright—Colorado's golden hour never failed to impress. Yet, in the background, dense clouds still blanketed the sky.

We all went inside, and I greeted my two dogs, overjoyed that everyone was okay. A news channel was playing on the TV. We talked for a while about what happened when my parents asked about the events. As we explained, my dad intently listened to the details, while my mom shook her head in disbelief. I sat on the couch, still feeling those shocking waves of anxiety trace up and down my body. I tried to suppress it as much as I could for my family. It was difficult to even breathe.

My phone finally gained power again. My inbox on social media and SMS toppled with tons of messages from old friends, current friends, and family. It comforted me that I crossed their minds, but it was a lot to reply to. I had the same answer to the same question over and over.

"Yeah, I'm okay."

"I'm fine."

Even old friends from my elementary years and middle school asked me how I was doing. It baffled me to see that they cared out of nowhere. Why did it take a shooting to ask me how I was?

Hours passed as we talked. Everybody shared their experiences of what they went through.

Jimmy told his story first. He was at a gym by our house. He was exercising until all the screens changed to the news channel. The tiny screens bore the headline: "High school in Colorado attacked by two shooters." He thought nothing of it, maybe felt a tinge of worry or pity, but he began to recognize the area that the clips revealed. Then he saw the texts from us stuck at the school. That was when he realized it was our school that was under attack; it was our school that had the tragedy this time. He raced out of the gym to come to us. He showed up near the school when my dad told him to follow instructions from first responders instead. Lucky for us, just down the way from the school was a police station. The staff and police redirected families to a recreational center called Westridge first. There, they could wait for their child. He waited for hours in a crowded basketball court full of angry and worried parents. They would ask authorities for updates on where their child was, if they were safe, and who they were with. Needless to say, the situation was stressful and tense.

He told us that it took a while to reach us, but when he finally did, he was so relieved.

My mother went next. It was a regular day at work for her. She had shut off her phone because she was about to enter a meeting. She got the strange sense that we were texting her and felt a rippling anxiety. She asked the vice president in the meeting if she could leave, as she thought she wasn't needed. They allowed her, and her hunch was right. Immediate reports from the news popped up as well as notifications. She left her work in haste to get my little brother David first—she knew that Jimmy was already at Westridge to retrieve us. She called David, making sure he knew that she was coming for him. Once they came home, they both waited to watch updates on the situation.

For David, he was in school when they announced a lockout. Students could continue class and walk around, but nobody could leave the school. They pulled my little brother away to the office with the intent to keep him from hearing the news from a classmate. The principal notified him that STEM had a confirmed shooter and that we were in danger. David felt a shock; he had no idea it was happening at STEM. He went back to the music room with his classmates, with no source of updates except from texts and the jokes of his classmates. It was difficult for him that day due to the fact that his classmates insisted on being ignorant and jocular. His friend was trying to call her mom to see if he could stay with her for the night. My mom got there to pick him up, and he didn't have to stay elsewhere, luckily.

Luke and his partner were walking around the school to skip class. They stuck in the middle school area and talked to each other. Then, the two came across Alec. Luke's partner complained about an assignment to Alec and then added a deprecative joke about wanting to get shot. Alec might as well have pulled out the gun at that moment, but he stuck to the plan. After Alec left, it was only a few minutes until Luke was alone. A few students ran past before gunshots echoed down the hall. A room in the high school hall was nearby, and Luke ran inside, waiting with the rest in lockdown. The students heard shouts coming from the middle school. Words such as, "this is all your fault," most likely projected at a teacher. After sitting in wait for nearly an hour, everyone was evacuated outside. Luke and I reunited and stayed close after that.

We continued watching the news and became appalled by the lack of empathy the news reporters had. They would show kids and teachers crying, parents reuniting with their children, and first responders guarding the survivors in clips. But as the screen returned to the reporters, they seemed to be in the middle of a joke. I knew that I should never trust the media in times like these.

They then revealed one of the shooters. I had heard earlier that it was one minor and one adult. The adult's name was Devon Erickson. I felt shocked. I knew Devon because my best friend had a crush on Devon for years. I gave her advice to talk to Devon more and focus on getting him to date her. Guilt immediately instilled in my heart. I found out that the same friend was in the room that the shooting started in, and she escaped by herself.

We had no idea who the confirmed second shooter was yet. I heard it was Alec, and I was almost sure it was, but I felt mistrustful as it wasn't confirmed yet. I didn't want to believe it. I remember I kept looking for that logic and reason. I tried healing with my brain instead of my heart, and that damaged my healing process in immense ways. I never spoke of my emotions that day; I only spoke of politics and statistics and facts. I regret that.

If you ever find yourself in a situation like mine, please do not hesitate to talk with your heart. It is so important to start with your emotions when it comes to healing.

Every time I talked about the event, I felt shivers and anxiety crawl up and down my body. I ignored them the best I could and continued to feed my brain with the logistics and the pieces of the story.

It became dark, and Charlie finally came over. We were first in a somber mood, and I made sure he felt okay. Soon, we were talking about it again. He told me his experience, which scared me the most out of any experience I heard so far.

He described that he was in the elementary school gym for the AP test. The proctor, joined by the students, ran into a small storage closet to hide. There were no doors at the entrance of the gym, so it would be unsafe to stay out in the open. They crammed inside the storage closet like sardines without a proper lock. To add, their phones weren't with them because of their test.

The proctor braced against the door to hold it closed; they all flinched upon hearing the gunshots nearby. They stood in wait before hearing loud footsteps and a bang. A police officer knocked down the door, sending the small proctor flying across the room. They all came out unharmed. Charlie was unable to get his phone as he was led out. He also told me he prepared to fight back, and that was something that made me frightened. He might've been another casualty and it saddened me—especially as the gym was such a large and open space where it's easy to find and kill.

We were soon all on my living room couch, playing a racing game. I felt happy and comforted that he was there. We had some funny moments—David cuddled next to Charlie while trying to beat him at the race. I felt twinges of loneliness as they stuck close. It felt difficult to even get up for a snack, just because I never wanted to let Charlie out of my sight again. We laughed and enjoyed the fact that we were together, safe, and alive.

Yet, that night, I struggled to sleep. The anxiety was crawling into me again. Flashes of what happened before came rushing little by little. I didn't know why, but that was the way I processed it. One moment I'd be fine, and the next, I would crash in desperation and cry. It was a difficult time.

It happened because I felt with my mind instead of my heart. I didn't want to accept that it happened just yet. It felt as if every time

I seemed fine, my mind would remind me I wasn't. I would shake and experience the fear all over again; how uncertain I was, how my heartbeat was in my throat, and especially how I had to keep it together for the children I kept company with. From the beginning, I viewed this tragedy as something stoic. Ever since I held back tears of fright for those kids, I thought it would be best to only think about the shooting in a concrete manner. I didn't want to be emotional about it at all. I absorbed all the information I could and ignored the fact that I went through something terrible. I constantly conspired and theorized what happened exactly when I was hiding away, in the dark about what went on. I suffocated my emotions in a bottle and shoved them aside, only taking them out when I felt it was appropriate—when I needed to sympathize while supporting a friend.

The week after the shooting, I hated emotion. I didn't want to be defined or characterized by what happened to me. I felt alone and scared. Yet, I was foolish and wanted to put up the front of someone who was strong in the face of adversity.

CHAPTER 4

It wasn't very long until they announced the name of the student who got shot. Kendrick Castillo jumped in front of the shooter to take him down. His courageous sacrifice saved me and so many others. A couple of others, Brendan Bialy and Joshua Jones, got injured as they jumped to protect as well. The rest chose to remain unnamed, but a couple more in the room also assisted in taking down the gunman.

The very next day, two memorial services were announced. One was at a Methodist church in remembrance of Kendrick Castillo. The other was at a high school nearby, but we weren't sure of its intentions. Our family went to the first without hesitation, and Charlie joined us.

It was a beautiful service. I saw many of my friends and teachers, and I was able to cry with them and experience the reassurance provided.

They sang worship songs and gave us advice and help. We were able to eat afterward and talk and mourn. Upon mentioning Kendrick's sacrifice, everyone stood and applauded for two minutes.

It was an amazing service that comforted many of us.

Many can agree that the second was not the same.

At the end of the first service, a handful of my friends were planning to go to the memorial service at the high school. Luke and I gained interest, but he went first, and I stayed behind. The rest of us ended up going anyway—especially since David needed a ride home from his school musical, which he played the lead in.

At first, I looked around for David and concluded that we needed to wait for his musical to be over. There were stairs by the entrance that led to the gym, which I assumed was where the memorial was taking place. It piqued my interest so I snuck in. I saw some of my friends cradling each other, having fresh tears staining their faces. Luke tossed a plush squirrel at me, and I received the small notion of comfort with thanks.

I was with Charlie as well, so we made our way to find some seats. A politician was talking at the podium, but we already knew something wasn't right.

He spoke of protecting our lives and keeping us safe. Yet, he was quick to insert his political intentions with gun laws and restrictions. We felt our peace being disturbed, but we regained it for a second as a different speaker lined up. It was a woman speaking, yet again, about politics and trying to relate to the victims of the shooting.

I looked around and saw news cameras everywhere. I found it peculiar but decided to go along with it. As long as they wouldn't record me or my family, I was fine. They taped the choir kids who sang some cheap gospel songs about hope and redemption. I realized that it wasn't an event organized by the STEM community at all. Rather, it was by an obscure group that only cared about politicizing victims of gun violence. They tried convincing us to vote for a representative or a law because we went through a traumatizing event.

As the woman spoke, we felt unquestionably bored and irritated by their lack of sympathy. My ludicrous friend then shouted, "let the STEM kids speak!"

Everyone cheered and agreed. The woman speaking seemed appalled by our ability to stand up for ourselves. She stammered on the microphone and then attempted to talk to one of the organizers to see if one of us could speak. They came to the conclusion that a few kids could speak. They asked whoever wanted to speak to stand up and go outside, so they could organize who would speak when.

After a handful of students left, they turned off the lights and asked us to light up our phones' flashlights. We felt content that we could finally get our voices heard. We all hummed a gospel song and sat in peace. We mourned the death of Kendrick, and the suffering we had all gone through. I leaned on Charlie and thought to myself, *If I was so lucky to be alive, why was I going through political games? Have I become another statistic?*

My thoughts got interrupted by a shaken woman who came up to the microphone and began to speak.

"I'm so sorry. . . but, um, the students who were about to speak—"

"We can't hear you!" a student shouted, and the women began to speak louder with a shaky voice.

"We're unable to provide student speakers, because the media—"

The crowd didn't let her finish. Instant shouts of denial and booing rose from students sitting on the bleachers.

She kept trying to excuse the fact that they were silencing us. She blamed the media and said they took the student speakers. Charlie booed along with the crowd, and I followed him as we walked out with Luke. Still, I was disoriented and confused. Everyone seemed to be moving at once—cameramen, speakers, and students alike—in one big blur of emotion. The organizers attempted to calm the enraged students and tried to get them seated again. Yet, they bundled together outside in a crowd. Their flashlights shone on in the dark to see if the media took away any students, or if the woman was lying. Groups of students stood up at once, filtering out of the gym as the staff tried to rationalize with them. Charlie pulled me out with him as I still knew nothing about what was going on, or why they were mad. Was it because of the tacky gospel music? Maybe it was because of the way the woman interrupted the moment of silence for Kendrick. Nevertheless, I knew something was wrong, and I knew that the STEM kids would do everything in their power to show how upset they were.

Once outside of the gym doors, Charlie, Luke, and my mom were stuck in the middle of it all. They had the right to be angry. The intention of that organization was to politicize and use students. They all chanted "mental health" as they marched outside. It was a rightful chant. The event completely disregarded healing and support for students.

My brother David greeted us with a smile on his face and a celebratory wreath around his neck, ornate with single dollar bills and candy. The smile soon disappeared as he realized his surroundings. David—I completely forgot—had his musical that same evening, and it was opening night.

I told him we had to get out as soon as possible to avoid any sudden protests. Not only would our presence intensify the crowd further, but it would also increase our disorientation and frustration. Charlie and I led him outside so that we could find my father's car to drive away. We hoped to separate from the uprising of the STEM students. A crowd began to form in front of the entrance of the high school. They shouted words of empowerment, such as "we are STEM" and other slogans. "Not a statistic" and "you should feel ashamed" became audible as well.

I tried to focus on David as we wandered through the dark parking lot, our direction misguided. The air was cold and dry; it began to drizzle snow and rain, making that May evening all the more bizarre.

I asked David how opening night was, but he seemed distracted by the events that were taking place. We explained the anger of the students and how the uprising took place. He described how awful he felt that the musical's opening night was just *a day* after the incident. I agreed that they should've rescheduled the musical to another time. There he was, celebrating with a bright pink wreath on his neck and leftover stage makeup while traumatized students were crying and shouting in protest. Familiar faces bustled through the crowd, tears staining their cheeks as they searched for friends.

We panicked as we couldn't find my father's car and continued to try for minutes at a time. All the while, the shouting from the protest grew even louder.

Finally, we spotted the distinct headlights and all climbed into the car. We were all so glad to be finally driving away and going somewhere more peaceful.

Of course, we couldn't forget David's success at the school musical, so we asked him how a pancake place sounded and we all agreed to go.

On the drive, we explained to my dad what exactly was happening, and why the students got enraged. On social media, I could see many status updates and new slogans coming about, such as "we are STEM" and "STEM strong." I, too, became enraged due to the fact I was being used as a pawn in their political game.

The rest of the night was as normal as it could get. We reached the restaurant and ate with David to celebrate opening night, at least as much as we could. A few students from STEM came by, and Luke and I spoke with them about the protests for a couple of minutes.

Later that night, news reports showed footage of the event at the high school, and how the evening derailed into a mess of emotion and trauma, and then later developed into a snug and commemorative get-together. I watched how the rest of the night went at the high school in eagerness. Luckily, students spoke at the podium. Friends and family gathered in a circle around it, wrapping arms around each other. They spoke of healing and of the sacrifices made. They remembered the victims and used the freedom to speak up.

Political manipulation might have worked at another school, or another group of hurt kids, but not STEM. STEM is a school of smart leaders who never let people take advantage. Even when we got forced into a vulnerable and hurt state, we rose to action.

I will always keep STEM as a part of me no matter where I go and no matter what I do. I respect those kids who stood up for themselves and didn't allow any trampling by the media or politics. Later that night, I read fresh news articles that showcased speeches from the students after the protest. I saw posts on social media about the uprising, and how they refused to be pushed down and pitied. Those were touching and only intensified the feeling of connection to my peers.

On Thursday, May 9th, I remember going to a nearby restaurant and feeling the worst I've ever felt. I was sitting with David, Luke, and my mother, my heart sinking in my chest as we ate. My mom attempted to pull words out of us. Yet, I found it inappropriate to speak about anything other than the shooting. We ate in depressive silence.

A handful of preppy students walked in at one point. They were laughing, talking, and glancing at the sad stock we were. I tried to ignore them, but I couldn't eat in peace while they stared. I felt ashamed of the STEM stickers on my wallet and phone. I felt pitied. I soon became angry at this, and we left as soon as possible.

A couple hours passed and one of Luke's friends came over. He then told us about his experience with the shooting—it was difficult to talk about anything else.

He was in math class, which was the last class of the day. The teacher had no idea of what was going on, so he reassured the students that it was only a drill. Various shouts and police chatter rose in volume. They became unsure whether it was a drill or not. Then, all of the sudden, someone came by their classroom and begged them to let him in. They were all unsure of what to do, but they kept away from the door and made sure they didn't open it. They heard the kid outside scream as police came up to take him. The kid was Devon.

Luckily, Devon dropped his gun in the classroom he started in. He began to run from Mrs. Harper's room all the way upstairs to the high school. He tried to escape from the police by rattling the doorknob and knocking over and over again. He shouted, begging to get into the math classroom.

My head felt relieved that I received this piece of information. I was confused hearing middle school students joke about people knocking on doors and encouraging others to go outside. Maybe they heard this story from the grapevine, and it got twisted through word of mouth. In any case, it would prove useful in putting everything together, but my heart felt heavy.

Later that day, I found out the full story and completed a version in my head.

Reports say that the both of them did drugs before entering the school after lunch break. It started in the middle school area, in Mrs. Harper's room, where I saw Alec before it all happened. Devon entered the classroom with a guitar case and Alec with his backpack. The two entered the room from different doors. In an interview, he told officials that he fired each weapon he had until they were empty. Then, he ran out of the room, getting the last gun out with intent to kill himself. He tried to pull the trigger, but the safety got left on. Before he could shoot himself, an officer came and tackled him.

For Devon, in Mrs. Harper's room, once he entered, he set his things down. Then he got back up again and locked the door. In a few moments, he pulled out his gun and stood in front of everybody, asking them not to move. A handful of brave souls jumped at Devon to attack him and disarm him. According to interviews they did a month after with Devon, he didn't mean to shoot Kendrick. He shot out of fear as they attacked them. Bullets left the classroom through the walls, harming students in the room adjacent. Quite a few friends I had who were in that room managed to escape due to their sacrifice. For that, I am thankful. After Devon left his gun, Kendrick began bleeding out. Devon sprinted out of the room in escape. The police already received an emergency call, so it was all a waiting game. Devon ran to the math room in desperation, attempting to get in. From there, he got detained. The security guard actually fired, which injured a female student in a classroom nearby, and then shot twice at a police officer. The threat was neutralized, and those injured went to hospitals. Everyone self-evacuated or evacuated with officials.

In dangerous situations, you remember *everything* you sensed. I remember the faint smell of dust and the arid scent of circulated air. I remember the dark faces in the room illuminated slightly by the blue light coming from the windows. I remember my hands grasping on the scratchy classroom carpet every now and then to alleviate the sweat coming from my hands. Yet at the same time, it all seems like a blur. My sense of time was warped; I wasn't sure how to organize the pieces in my mind. That is why many parts of the story are confusing or seem out of place. At the time, all that mattered was piecing it all together and getting the right story to tell. In retrospect, I realized it doesn't matter how it happened—what matters is that it did.

Reading countless news reports, I learned that Devon claimed he didn't want to hurt anybody. He had a panic attack minutes before the incident, which stopped him from telling a teacher. Even while pleading innocent in a court of law, I still find him guilty in my eyes.

I wasn't prepared in any way for the reaction of the community I would soon face when I came in contact with them. For now, it was the sweet stability and comfort of the STEM community. I had no idea the pity I would face up front once I ventured outside.

CHAPTER 5

It was already Friday, May 10th, three days after the shooting. Dark clouds blanketed the sky, and it was terribly windy. In fact, it had been like this for the whole week. I didn't think much of it back then—Colorado is notorious for having rapid changes and differences in weather. Yet, in hindsight, it seemed like a sign that things were dark, but eventually, they would become bright again. In fact, it already seemed brighter—I was planning to hang out with some of my friends, Hannah and Mandy, along with Charlie. We wanted to see David's musical, a formal production from his school. It was the same school I went to for almost seven years. I was nervous to see the reaction of my old teachers and peers once they met me.

First, though, I was going to get my hair dyed.

I went to the salon and showed my stylist the picture that replicated what I desired for my hair. She colored it and washed it, but she offered for someone else to style my hair later on. Oh no, I thought, I was just fine here. It's not like the style would have been any different anyhow. Plus, one look at the stylist, and I could already tell she'd talk about something personal.

The stylist was quick to ask me the question I'd been dreading.

"What school do you go to?" she asked as she tugged on my hair.

I paused briefly, making a decision. "STEM," I said logically, as if it was a simple and normal school with no history. I didn't want any pity or concern or apologetic looks.

"Oh. . . I'm sorry," she replied, regardless of my internalized wishes. Why do people apologize for things they didn't do? I assured her with a shrug and nearly muttered, "It's okay."

She began to further inform me of her past with Columbine and how she graduated from there. She never specified if she was a victim or not, but I was too angry to sympathize. I peered endlessly at myself in the mirror in front of me. I expressed my dissatisfaction with a dropped face as I wondered again why it had to happen to my school. Before any of this happened, when I told people I went to STEM, they asked me where it was, even what it was. They asked if I studied robotics there, and in retrospect, I long for the innocence of telling people I studied language arts instead. Now it was on the map, and not in a good way. I guarantee, if someone types "STEM School" in a search bar, a majority of the results will mention the shooting, or Devon, or Alec. I've always wanted the world to recognize my school, but not in this way. It was unfortunate for me and my peers to experience, especially when trying to heal. My pride for the school only deteriorated this way.

Imagine someone asked you where you went to school, or where you went to work. Now imagine instead of their approval or interest as an initial reaction, it's pity. I'd describe it as a face they'd give to you if you told them your cat died.

It's frustrating, especially as STEM was a second home. It was the place I was so eager to go to because I wanted to learn and hang out with my friends. I didn't see it as a surface-level tragedy like others outside the community did.

I got home after I finished at the salon and met with Charlie. I saw Hannah and Mandy, who were a couple of the outsiders who worried about me with sincerity. I appreciated them because they were polite and understanding. We all prepared to go to see David perform in his school musical.

I didn't expect to face the reactions of old classmates, teachers, and mentors. I knew they cared for me, it just felt fake, especially due to the topic's recency. I already faced one the day prior when picking David up from his second night performing. An old teacher and mentor of mine began preaching to me about the "tragedy at STEM and in the community"—as if I didn't know.

I respect that they were most likely affected by it as well, seeing an old student or classmate of theirs put in danger like that. Still, I did not need to have constant reminders of what I faced that day, much less nod along to their ramblings on how terrible they felt about it.

I was livid that night. Not to mention that students from other schools were using this tragedy to their advantage. They all said that they were so affected, as the shooting happened five miles away from their school. Students in those schools even claimed falsely on live television that they saw dead bodies . It made no sense to me—but they were obviously doing it for attention.

I prepared myself with a deep breath before entering the high school again. I could remember the protest chants of angered students and the yelling and crying from the night of the "vigil." This time, though, I was with people I loved—not separated from them as I tried to find them through a bustling crowd.

We entered the auditorium. I looked around for old teachers, trying to hide away in my seat as fast as possible. I still wore a bracelet that quoted "#STEMstrong" along with stickers on my wallet and phone. Looking back, I didn't know why I was so scared if I bore those stickers and bracelets in front of the public with pride. I definitely didn't want to boast about the trauma I had experienced. Perhaps it felt like a subconscious obligation to wear those stickers with pride—otherwise, I'd seem disloyal. My feelings about the community had its highs and lows. There were days—like the night of the vigil—where my support and connection were at an all-time high. But other times, I felt ostracized from other kids my age, like the day I went to a restaurant with my siblings and felt ashamed in front of the preppy students.

I stayed with my friends for a little while. Yet, I longed to meet up with my teachers again. They felt worried for me, so what could be the harm in meeting up with them? I knew I was assuming, relating that one teacher's response to everyone else's. Sure, the majority treated me like a poor beaten animal, but I couldn't assume that would be the general reaction.

I joined Jimmy as he spoke to my old gym teacher. The teacher didn't jump straight into the topic of STEM—instead, he asked me how my siblings were, how my dogs were, and other casual questions. Then he asked me the question about that fateful day. I've been asked a million times and have been expecting it ever since. There's a look in their eyes after greeting me as they glance around expectantly and pause. I sat in all conversations, holding my breath as if underwater, just waiting for those words.

"Are you okay?"

I reassured him that I was doing fine, and that the community was healing. I tried mentioning things that were positive. Maybe a change in perspective might help people with their outlook on STEM and its community.

The first encounter wasn't so bad! I said hello to a few others before the show started, including my teachers from eighth grade. Again, they were sensitive, and they didn't jump right into the topic of the shooting. Instead, they complimented my new hair and told me about how proud they were of David. Then, they asked if I was okay, and I told them I was. But they never dove into the topic like others did earlier. They also refrained from explaining their points of view or inquiring about specifics, which I appreciated.

The musical was amazing and I had an immense amount of fun. It was pleasant to distract myself for a little while, I suppose, as the whole week was about STEM. They did mention in the beginning that they were there for STEM and expressed they were "STEM strong." Usually, I would cringe or scoff, but I smiled to myself and felt it was thoughtful, especially because of my history with the school.

We went home, and David explained how good it felt to finally be over with the show. It was fun, he said, but to have it right after the shooting was an extreme downer. I sympathized with him. He had to put on a mask and act as a happy character the day after his friends and siblings were put in imminent danger. It made me feel so sorry—it must've hurt him.

For a while, I always prioritized my feelings and the way I hurt. Yet I never thought of how it hurt David, as I know he's the type to brush things off and stand up as soon as he can. He expressed how his peers and teachers made him feel awful for wanting to go to STEM, even after the shooting.

His pride for the school surpassed mine. Even my family felt ashamed. Unfortunately, I did too.

CHAPTER 6

A couple days passed since David's performance. I had to face the same community again for his graduation from 8th grade. The fact that I was acting as if I had pride in STEM didn't help out as much as I thought it would—it felt suffocating. I gave myself no room for feeling. A spotless victim, that's what I wanted to be. I filled whatever empty patches I had with STEM pride stickers and words of rationalization.

All my siblings and I went to the charter school David was graduating from. It was a K-8—so we were all practically raised there. They have a tradition of letting the eighth graders walk outside on a red carpet to complete their year. It's accompanied by a decadent walk-out theme song, as family members watch standing in the hall before the entrance. It's like a rite of passage, since 8th grade was the highest grade, making them the top dogs of the school. It probably was the last time they would feel like alphas until they reached senior year in high school. Hence, it was crowded and packed with families of the students. More importantly, families I knew.

I gave into my mom's begging with reluctance, as she wanted me to attend the singular event. It was only me and my mom, as the real event—the graduation ceremony—happened later in the evening.

I didn't feel too afraid of potential pity, but it dampened my mood at times. I still wasn't going to let that ruin David's walk-out or his formal graduation.

Some staff members I used to know came up to me and asked how I was doing and attempted to sympathize. I appreciated their efforts, but it seemed like they were over-exerting their worry at the moment. A few more gave me the "your cat died and I pity you" face, but it wasn't as bad.

It was finally warmer that day. I wore a morose and blank face around others so that they wouldn't approach me. Some knew better than to do that at this point—they'd only bother me if it was a part of the conversation. We walked out to greet David as he finished his red carpet walk. The crowd of students and family felt overwhelming, but I kept a brave face for David. His classmates were crying about missing each other as they took pictures. I didn't remember my red carpet walk being that emotional. It must've been a closer class.

We all got into the car as I expressed my eagerness to leave the event. I needed alone time before the graduation event later on. I began to feel overwhelmed and avoidant due to the red carpet walk. I disliked the idea of staying longer because I knew they would push a conversation with me—and I wanted anything but that.

David told my mom to wait as we came up to the exit of the school. He was patting his pockets aimlessly, claiming he had lost his phone. My mom parked and told him to hurry. She must've sensed that I was getting tense.

My mom instructed me to step inside and help David find his phone. He mentioned leaving it in his math classroom, a place I knew well from my eighth grade year there. As I brushed past parents and students in the hall, I saw my old math teacher. She intercepted my hurried search for David, clearly wanting to talk to me. I was embarrassed. I remembered doing one-on-one tutoring sessions with her. I felt ashamed, especially since I knew that she hoped I would do well. Truth was, I wasn't doing well. Back then, as her student, I was noticeably content, even if it didn't physically show—short frizzy hair, poorly done eyeliner, and an affinity for wearing baggy, covering clothes. I was naïve and in a coming-of-age mentality. We never conversed much in the past—but having even shorter, dyed hair and my expression darkened by recent events, one would find difficulty being remiss. She must've seen the difference and had been taken aback upon approaching me.

She asked me how I was and I claimed I was doing fine, though it seemed like she asked simply because she was curious. She didn't ask, "How are you doing?" or, "Are you okay?" It was a simple and genuine, "How are you?" To others, it might seem trivial to place such importance on a difference like that, but it meant all the world to me. She saw me, not my recent difficulties or newly attained trauma.

I told her what was going on with David, and she told me she would check in her classroom. She returned telling me that she couldn't find it, but wished me luck on the search. As I turned, she tapped my shoulder and suggested that I return to my mom's car, so they wouldn't end up looking for me once David found his phone. Logistically, it would put us in more confusion to have two people looking at the same time in different places, so I followed her advice and made my way back to the car.

As I walked back, another old teacher offered to walk me back, putting a forceful, leading arm around my shoulder. He closed the distance and began asking in hushed tones the same inquiries. Was I okay, how is the school doing, droning on with his inquiries and concern. I nodded along and reassured him I was fine. Honestly, it seemed wrong that I was the one comforting outsiders instead of being comforted by them. It was even more ironic, because they thought their exaggerations and constant questions were consoling. I get it, they needed answers—but honestly, why couldn't I catch a break?

I finally entered the car and sighed, half out of relief and half out of distress. We were stuck in the front of the drive-line as we waited for David to return with his lost phone. The staff outside was directing cars to drive around us in order to leave. At this point, I already had enough with the fake sympathy and pity. David was taking a while to search for his phone. Alas, yet another old teacher of mine was assisting my mother while we waited, hovering her head before the open window next to the passenger seat. I sat between my mom and her, crossing my arms and listening to their pleasantry.

I glanced briefly at her face. I could see it in her expression. After a little bit of restraining from the topic, she couldn't resist. I know my teachers and peers had good intentions. Yet every time they tried to talk to me, it seemed like overdone sympathy. Hence, why I felt the immense amount of pity I received from others.

Anyhow, the conversation went something like this:

"And how are you?" Her expression was tilted upward as she asked.

"I'm okay, getting better."

"Oh, yeah? That's good. How's your sibling?"

"Fine."

"I'm so sorry about what happened. It seemed like such a good school!"

Seemed? That was when I snapped at her.

"You know, STEM is still a good school. They're trying their best." My tone was unwavering and prickly—I had no politeness left in me, I could only handle so much. I was done with the assumptions for the day.

She clarified that she was never trying to incriminate the school or make it seem like it was their fault. Yet I hated hearing the same undertone every time. Everyone always jumped to conclusions and pitied me. None of us ever expected it or could have known.

In hindsight, I realize I could have been nicer to the people offering sympathy—but ever since the first person pitied me, I felt like a fragile victim. The one who you can't touch lest you want them to crumble onsite. I felt like I needed to be strong and act like I was completely fine. I wanted to show them that I went through a tragedy, but I wasn't a tragic outcome. It made the healing process even more of a struggle. I didn't allow myself to be vulnerable or to feel in the correct way. I didn't consider my emotions; I would appear weak to the people around me.

We drove away as David came back, and we all felt relieved to get away from such enormous social pressure.

Charlie later joined us to come to David's graduation. I felt better going to these things with inner support—someone who understood what I went through—going with me. It was the beginning of us bringing each other everywhere. We found peace and safety whenever we were together. It was a crucial time for our relationship, as we both needed each other's solace. Thankfully, Charlie never had much of a negative reaction. He stood and brushed himself off quickly, still managing to keep sympathy and remembrance in mind. It was lucky for me because after what happened, I fell apart. I had little strength and kept lying to myself about everything. I kept telling myself I had to be strong, even in front of family. I kept telling myself I wasn't valid as a survivor because my experience wasn't as bad as other experiences.

When I was with Charlie, though, I could be a mess. I could be stone cold and rigid or blubbering and tearful. He has and always will be my rock. I usually had him to rely on if I ever got angry at the world. I would fixate on daily occurrences far too often, especially if they were related to instances of pity from the outside community. I would get upset, not knowing why—but I knew that Charlie would be there, and I could at least rely on that.

The graduation event was held at a prestigious high school's amphitheater nearby. It was a beautiful ceremony. Very few peers and teachers brought up the shooting, to my surprise. It was most likely because they already expressed their sympathies and apologies earlier.

The night went well. The cake I had was amazing too. I found myself reserved from conversation, especially with people I knew well. I stuck by Charlie's side as he came along and pretended to seem occupied or distracted with him when needed.

A significant event happened for me that night.

We were at a restaurant, making stupid jokes with each other— something about a pea on a table. It was the first time in a long while that I laughed so hard my stomach hurt. I felt emotional that night—I realized I did bottle up not only sad and angry emotions but also the happy ones. That evening truly felt like a summer night—colorful and golden.

Looking back, it was the pressure of the community and the survivor's guilt that convinced me I didn't have the right to feel happy. Everyday needed to be angry, tense, and depressing in memory of what happened.

I know that is not what Kendrick Castillo would have wanted, so I'm glad I found the joy to laugh again.

After that night, I challenged myself to find the joy in things and focus on the positive.

CHAPTER 7

It was now more than a week after the shooting. My siblings and I went to hear the experience of a Columbine survivor. Quite a few people came to this event that students organized. They had snacks and water for the students who came.

We all sat down and got settled as the Columbine survivor began to speak. It was an inspirational talk for me. Finally, somebody who actually understood! All this time, I had been receiving overdone lectures from people who had no idea what we felt.

She spoke of her experience in Columbine and the death of her best friend, Rachel. She also spoke on how many people wanted to exploit her experience for the media. When she mentioned exploiting, it resonated with many of us. Most of the time, the media portrayed the tragedy in a completely insensitive way. Their only intent, I have reason to believe, was to use our experience to have more views on what they produced.

I had an experience with this several times. One time, a journalist contacted me in a very polite manner through my social media. It felt unexpected. My experience with the media so far was simple insensitivity. The journalist asked if I wanted to "have my voice heard" during an interview for an article. I asked my father for his suggestion and he told me not to.

At the time, I held a grudge against him for limiting me, but he was right. Why would I want to be even more of a spectacle, or a show of pity? Some people I knew participated, and it seemed harmless. A majority of it focused on the interviews rather than what was written by the journalist, and for that I'm grateful. Yet, I'm glad I stayed away from participation. It was more of an unnecessary showcase, and who knew if my perspective was going to be twisted?

The meeting with the Columbine survivor was a relief from the tension of the community. I left early, though my two other siblings stayed. They started speaking of post-traumatic stress disorder and I felt as if I didn't belong. What right did I have to say that I felt traumatized by the sounds of gunshots when I didn't hear any at all?

I know my feelings were valid as well as my trauma. It was the survivor's guilt, once more, that made me feel like the odd one out. I suppose I didn't want to offend anybody by saying I got traumatized. Yet I still get scared of loud sounds and crowds, and feel as if I'm in danger once more.

I felt overwhelmed from everything that was being said. I felt that intense and anxious feeling—shivering, holding in tears, perspiring—so I decided to leave early when there was a break.

I contacted friends and checked up on them, fishing to hear more experiences. I sought out the stories of others, more than I should have, and I thought it would help me process and heal.

I told them my experience in return. Anxiety still made my legs lock up and freeze, even if I was texting and not speaking aloud.

They told me it must have been frightening. I agreed, but deferred and said I was thankful I didn't hear anything.

Then they reminded me of the fear I had felt, not knowing what was going on, the suspense, and fear taking over. The reality of putting a strong front for the children made it worse. I empathized with many teachers once I realized that I was put in a similar position.

That is why I found my experience unique from my peers who most likely had the comfort of their classmates. The two classmates I was with weren't super close friends. Plus, they were not the best to cuddle up to out of fear, seeing that they did not seem very affectionate.

The same events transpired at home every time I went back. I have to admit, I despised coming home each night. I knew I would come back to the same situation where we talked about the incident whenever available. In short, it wasn't ideal for me.

Each night was exhausting and restless. When I faced the tragedy, I kept wondering why someone like Alec would commit such a crime.

Many unofficial support systems popped up for STEM students. New connections, friendships, and a sense of familiarity spread across the community. We made each other family in light of the shooting.

The next few weeks were days of guilt and sorrow. Yet, there was understanding and community. I often saw single magpies. I remember when my family reassured me that it was most likely the weather, but I was sure it meant more. Superstition has always played a large role in my life—even when I was little, I used to notice magpies and count them, before I knew of the poem. Single magpies, meaning sorrow, were an often occurrence after the shooting. It used to fill me with dread, but when I saw them, I usually just noticed and moved on. It happened too often for me to care.

It was the day of Kendrick's memorial of life. My father promised us we would go to some sort of funeral for Kendrick once the time came. The closest we got to a funeral was a memorial of life open for the public. It was at a church, and invites went out to everybody in the community.

It was a beautiful service where we spoke of life. We recognized how amazing Kendrick was as a student and as a person in general. I was remorseful in the face of shaken friends, teachers, and family speaking to the community of STEM. Even the teacher who was in the room where Devon and Alec began shooting spoke. She seemed happy in an odd way, a gracious and peaceful contentment I couldn't define myself.

The service was nothing short of extraordinary. I found myself in an odd position of numbed joy. I didn't cry throughout all the touching speeches. I found peace when I looked at Kendrick's face on the pamphlet. His life was beautiful, filled with perpetual joy and an air of sainthood. He surrounded himself with happiness and loving people.

His parents mentioned at one point how his sacrifice was something he would unquestionably do. My family often reminded me that if there was a heaven, Kendrick would go there without a doubt, which comforted me.

Throughout everything Kendrick's parents went through, they offered support to the community. Comfort, hospitality, hugs—and they meant it. I respect them for these notions of kindness. They, too, have an aura of sainthood.

After the ceremony, they led us to the food. I didn't eat much as I focused on greeting friends. We hugged, talked, spoke about the beautiful service, and enjoyed each other's presence.

My parents and older brother went ahead to talk to the Castillos. I stepped outside for a moment of solitude.

It was a beautiful patio, elevated so that you could stare at the mountains. At that time of day, a sunny spell had occurred. Little spots of sunshine peeked through the dark clouds, giving out a refreshing air of peace. I remember when I asked my mother about sunny spells as a child, she would tell me that it meant a new soul entered heaven. To me, it was a sign that everything would be okay.

A week or so after, we had the chance to retrieve our belongings from the school, as it wasn't allowed before. They blocked off rooms for investigation and closed down the school. I came with my mother to retrieve my backpack, which I left in the music room. My mom was an emotional mess and I don't blame her. She cried upon seeing certain teachers and counselors, which I didn't understand then. Now I know it must've been scary to come to the place where your children were in danger.

We followed a teacher to the music room where I left my backpack. They organized it such that only a handful of kids would go at a time. I walked in, nonchalant, but I remember getting chills as I walked through the halls. I eyed the posters that claimed support and the cute sticky notes plastered on lockers and walls. I went to retrieve my backpack, nervous about how I'd feel. I noticed the lip balm peeking outside the side pocket. It angled the slightest bit to the left—exactly how I left it. My eyes filled with tears and my head raced with questions of where it went wrong. I picked up my backpack and stood beside my mom to embrace her. I felt numb in my emotions, yet confused and sorrowful at the same time.

Later that day, a student fainted and he got carried away in an ambulance. As the emergency services arrived, I couldn't help but notice everyone's expression. They turned to look where the sirens came from. Their faces filled with dread, unease, and numbness.

We left, but my gut twisted as I noticed the blocked off areas in the school and the scared faces. Maybe not everything was just as I left it.

The days after that, we had the chance to go back to school. It was optional, of course, but I went anyway for the last two days. The halls seemed bleak, no longer filled with joy. Familiar faces that once lit up the hallways looked down or glanced to the sides with pursed lips and blank eyes.

Most of the day, I was away from optional classes helping Charlie and a couple of his Boy Scout friends with an Eagle project. The assignment was to record the whole class singing a touching song Charlie wrote on living on even after tragedy happened. I walked to the elementary school—the part of the school where I hid in a room during the incident. I remembered how I was away from my friends, shaking and trying to keep tears in. I became nervous and had to excuse myself to sit elsewhere. There was a small lounging area next to the stairs where I sat huddled to myself. While I sat, I saw a handful of kids in a room with a teacher. They looked innocent and big-eyed and determined to learn despite what happened to them. I envied them. I wanted to be happy and eager. I hated the fact that it happened to me, and more importantly, that I understood too much of what happened.

I felt lonely in class despite being with friends. From those moments I spent back in the school, I knew it would be painful to come back to school next year. It would hurt me to try to focus on my studies. I never wanted to admit that it would be tough. But it *was* gonna be tough. I felt determined to be there for my friends and community always, even if it would kill me. Even if I didn't go to STEM. In all honesty, I'm glad I didn't. It would've broken me to keep smiling and pretend like I felt safe when I didn't.

I saw in a yearbook that they still had Devon's face at the end and a senior quote to match. I felt utter disbelief, but I knew the kids in the yearbook club wouldn't have the power to change it if they tried.

CHAPTER 8

It's often typical of smaller children to be clueless about the bigger pieces of life. Social etiquette, how rain works, death. The first time I recall being confronted with it was when I was no more than five or six years old. Luke and I were in the car with our dad, just picking up David from preschool. When we were all in the car together, my dad began speaking to us.

"Look up at the sky."

It was nighttime then; the moon was a crescent shape with clouds slightly shrouding its light. I never saw the stars shine brighter than that night.

"I want you to remember this—when someone dies, just think of it as heaven gaining another star."

I didn't have much of a concept of what death was at the time, but somehow, it made sense. I saw two stars shine brightly next to each other next to the moon and pointed them out to my siblings.

"So, your grandma has become a star tonight," my dad remarked remorsefully, a weak smile painting his expression.

"I think I see her," David grinned gleefully and we nodded in agreement.

Once we went back home, we saw our mother sweeping weakly over the hardwood floors in the dim light. We went over to give her a hug, which caused her to promptly fall apart in tears.

When my parents spoke to the Castillos at the memorial, they later invited us to Kendrick's rosary mass. I felt so honored, but the Castillos already felt like family to us. So at the same time, it seemed like we needed to go.

It was a sunny afternoon. We made it over to the rosary mass, and I was not expecting at all what was inside.

I stared at the open casket as we made it to a pew. I could see the beginnings of his side profile—the round of his nose and his dark eyebrows. I saw John and Maria Castillo sit at the first pew. They seemed hushed and contemplative, wondering and asking questions without end. I couldn't see their faces. Even without the privilege of talking to them very often, I observed them and pondered on their nature.

Maria is one of the strongest people I have ever met. Her face always seemed to have a pondering yet mournful air about it when I saw her, sometimes never making eye contact but instead, staring out. Even so, she had a graceful and beautiful aura surrounding her. She seemed content and kind, and always forgiving. She left wisdom behind her wherever she went, hopeful and contemplative as always. She's a faithful woman indeed. She always looked after herself and her husband. She even looked after the strangers around her.

Now, John was the social and emotional part. He had wept many times, and whenever I saw him, his eyes were tearful and surrounded by red skin from crying. But how beautiful he was as a person, being the first to offer hospitality. He always had the strength to give comfort to so many others. His eyes were always determined; he was always active and ready to help others as Kendrick was. Seeing John was like seeing a mirror image of his son, both alike in so many ways, yet so different and unique.

The aura of this family felt similar to something sacred. Each part was kind in a perpetual way, and they always wanted to help. I admired their beauty amid the chaos of the world.

Yet, this peace I managed to obtain from making personal observations didn't last long. My family and I knelt and began to pray with everyone else. My feet grew cold as I dreaded facing Kendrick in his casket. It should have been me, I thought. It should have been me.

The thoughts came rushing back, and the ever-intensifying feelings of guilt and sorrow. As we all knelt there, my palms grew cold and clammy. I begged under my breath that we wouldn't go up to see John, Maria, and Kendrick. It would wrench my heart out.

It was looking pretty hopeful for me near the end. They were closing the prayer mass. I breathed out a sigh of relief, but then they invited us all to visit the Castillos by the altar. My siblings tried to reassure me after that and tell me it was my choice. But it was helpless; I didn't want to stay behind and regret my decision forever. I sat there, my eyes studying the interior of the church, from the crucifix, to the pews, to the altar. But most of all, I studied the people leaving their pews to get in line for the open casket.

Row by row, ten to sixteen individuals left each pew. They wiped tears from their eyes and prepared their words for John and Maria. Condolences, prayers, love. I had *zero* idea of what I would say to them. What do you tell two parents who just suffered the greatest loss from the worst tragedy?

The usher finally came by our pew. My mother told me I could opt out and wait. But I knew I wouldn't ever be able to forgive myself if I sat there, watching my family speak to the Castillos. So I went up there. The whole time I was in line, I kept overthinking what I would say to John and Maria. The line was slow-going and agonizing as people would waddle up a few inches at a time.

Everyone before me would kneel before the casket and pray, so I followed along with my siblings.

I was facing Kendrick. I was kneeling before him and studying the features of his face. Jimmy mentioned that Kendrick has very similar facial features to our family. He was right. From the thick brows to the round cheeks and tan skin, he looked familiar.

I didn't stay long, but his face seemed like a baby's. He seemed like he was only sleeping, peaceful and quiet. I whispered a "thank you" to him, just in case he was listening, a lump in my throat forming. I felt peaceful knowing I faced Kendrick. The air in the church was dry. The atmosphere hung with the sounds of small sniffs and hushed voices. I rose to my feet, not feeling afraid anymore of seeing him. I have a habit of overthinking about open casket services and ceremonies. I've only seen two open casket services so far, including Kendrick and one of a close family friend. It feels unnerving at first, but seeing Kendrick filled me with a sense of closure. Some friends from STEM, including Charlie, spoke of how they knew Kendrick.. Whenever that happened, I felt immense guilt knowing I knew Alec, the shooter, and not Kendrick.

I still couldn't believe it was his body. I was in the dream-like state they talk about, where I didn't cry or feel anything. I faced John and Maria with my family. I hugged Maria and then John, showing them the sincerest love I could. But the words I practiced in my head on the way up were gone now. I could only depend on what came to my mind at the moment.

I told them my condolences, and that their son saved me and my friends' lives. For people who just suffered an unbelievable loss, they seemed so kind and willing. I thought about it for a second—I thought about my selfishness and hypocrisy. I was so greedy for attention, yet never gave it to others. I shunned everyone out of my life, even my family, and denied help at the same time.

It became easier not to cry after visiting Kendrick's coffin. I hugged the two and left after my father talked to John for a bit.

I felt a calm wash over me as I walked outside. My conscience was clear now that I came face to face with Kendrick. It felt as if a weight was lifted off my shoulders. I had a twisted feeling, however. I felt it was unfair that I never knew him in person. I heard all of these great things about him—his accomplishments, his love for others, his helpful nature—yet I could never put a name to the face. At least a tangible one. I knew only the ghost of him. I felt like a disgrace, knowing I couldn't change it. Yet, I consoled myself, knowing his spirit was somewhere else, somewhere beautiful and well deserved.

There were sweet snacks served outside, such as cookies and brownies. We savored a few of them before we drove off. The air around us was hushed as we left. The sky was overcast, yet somehow, the sun still shone through.

It was truly scenic—like the sunny spell a few days prior, but the sun was now hidden away, still illuminating. I didn't want to believe Kendrick was another star that illuminated the sky. It sounded lonely, even if there were many stars. Their presence is there, but they appear and fade like a glimpse of hope. Instead, I envisioned that Kendrick appeared as a sunny spell—he was away, but his presence still shone everywhere around us, and the warm afterglow of his life still strikes the hearts of many.

This whole memorial experience taught me that Kendrick deserved remembrance. He will remain in my heart forever as a hero and a saint.

CHAPTER 9

The day for senior graduation didn't start very well. The weather was harsh, cold, and unforgiving, like a storm was brewing. I had a few friends who invited me to graduation parties and such the weeks prior. They were solemn events in most instances, but it was a rather peaceful experience to see the seniors finally graduating. It was also bittersweet, but not only because my friends were moving on. Sure, they would finally leave high school and become adults, which was the sweet part. But I'm sure nobody wants to undergo a school shooting and live to tell the tale.

I stopped believing in a "perfect high school experience" ever since the two vigils. Every other kid in high school feels excited from the start. They want to have fun, make new friends, buy a prom dress for several hundreds of dollars, and go out with a bang when they have to graduate. Not STEM kids, and definitely not me. Nothing felt special anymore after the shooting. Of course, to worry about going to high school and be nervous about graduating is normal. I felt numb, so to speak, like I could care less. Special rites had no weight; the so-called "next big step" was nonexistent; it didn't matter any longer for me. Thus, the graduation felt like an apathetic and anxiety inducing event, at least in the beginning.

One of my graduating friends got tickets for my siblings, and we were soon seated inside. Getting inside was a hassle. It was pouring rain, and freezing, and you had to wait in line to get inside. Not to mention the ignoramus who prevented my dad from parking near the entrance. It was unfortunate to experience that right before the ceremony.

As we waited, I saw a peek of the graduates eating pizza and having expressions of mellow happiness. They weren't jumping off the walls excited, but it felt justified.

After a while, they began walking to the dais. We all stood and watched them with the same contentment in our faces. I saw a few friends I knew, and I was happy that they were proud. It still poured like hell outside, so we were on the field that had a retractable ceiling over it. I warily scouted for possible emergency exits around the building.

The graduation was inspiring and still bittersweet. I felt immense pity for Kendrick's parents. It must've hurt knowing their son was so close to graduating and being successful, only for it to all end in death from a couple of idiots with guns. They kept a portrait of him in the first seat, accompanied with a wreath of flowers and several sashes. They made sure to mention him and his bravery on several occasions, and when they did, the audience rose to their feet to applaud for minutes at a time.

I made sure to cheer for my friends as they strutted to receive their diplomas with pride, even if they told the families and friends to wait to applaud until after everyone went. I couldn't resist—I was happy for them. I felt only pure joy for my friends.

Kendrick's best friend received Kendrick's diploma for him. Again, everyone cheered like crazy. It was emotional for us all.

I embraced a few friends and took a few pictures with them, happy to see them so proud and accomplished. Their pride was well deserved. Completing high school at STEM is no easy feat.

After a while, we began to leave, and I heard small voices note the snow. Wait, snow?

I went to see for myself and indeed, a blizzard washed over us. It was unfortunate that the seniors had snow on their first day of summer, but it was meaningful to me in a strange way. The snowy weather symbolized a divergent and unique experience for the seniors. Usually, sunny weather can be expected for a graduation—yet, we were met with something different. Having a good and memorable event for the graduating class meant a lot to me, and I definitely would've felt sour if the shooting was the only defining factor of their class.

The blizzard roared on as Luke went to hold the door open for people. People were smiling regardless of the snow in May, proud of their children and happy to see the community. After everyone passed by, we made it back to the car to drive home.

My family was tense on the way back. We were hungry and cranky, and the cold was biting. Plus, the relentless blizzard made it difficult to drive in, and not to mention the lack of winter coats due to the fact that we were not expecting a snowstorm in May.

The strangest thing was that I was not sad as I was before seeing my friends graduate. I was proud of them and almost felt pity that the shooting would forever be a part of them. However, there were so many things about them that meant so much more than a tragedy—like winning in TSA competitions or running an awesome school play. Heck, they even managed to push through the rest of their senior year without falling apart after the shooting. They were the glue of our community. The class of 2019 was the best class of STEM in my heart.

I came to realize that the events that happened on May 7th never hit me. I wanted to realize it and get through it, but an emotional journey like this never ceases. It's rapid, continuous, confusing, and beautiful all at the same time. It becomes a part of you, even if you try to suppress it and ignore it. I never realized this in full, and it's still a struggle to accept. I wanted (and still want) to become successful, not a sad sack who never healed from her trauma. I pushed myself too hard. I thought, *okay, I should feel safe at STEM again. I shouldn't let out my feelings because I don't need to. My trauma is not important because I wasn't anywhere near the gunshots. I shouldn't make a victim of myself.*

That last part was right in a way. I didn't want to overreact and make a victim of myself because, it's true, I am more than my trauma. I thought I could always figure things out on my own. I felt that I didn't need to feel sorry for myself because people said I should. I didn't need to focus on myself. I needed to help others before myself because only through assisting others, I could heal.

I thought of these things for quite a while—but it wasn't my obligation to be there for others when I needed to be there for myself. Sometimes, the way I thought of things didn't make total sense. Still, I would abide to survive and feel better about myself. I never vented about my feelings or talked to anyone—I wanted to seem strong and successful. I wanted to appear as a thriving survivor to the people I talked to. Of course, the thoughts always loomed in my brain, but I didn't want to be the stereotypical mope everyone else was. I didn't want to stay up late at night wondering why it had to happen to me.

I thought I already knew the answer. It was coincidental, that was all I believed. I could push aside those thoughts whenever I wanted to because they were insignificant to me. I didn't have the time to think for myself or even wonder why. I was numb. In fact, I made myself numb, so people could see me as strong even after what happened. I made myself seem nonchalant and undisturbed to make people admire my strength.

All this was because I felt scared. I felt scared that people would pity me. I felt scared I would receive judgments from others, and they would only care about my trauma, not me as a person. The trauma stuck to me, haunted me, and even made me scared of interaction. That was the biggest mistake of all—to let the trauma define me. Even if I denied it, the tag, bolded and hanging off of my arm, stuck there. "STEM kid," it read. I declared it everywhere. From social media to socializing with strangers. All I wanted was their approval, their applause, their affections. I hated it defining me, but I let it because it benefitted me. It gave me a false sense of happiness, of feeling like I was enough.

The poor STEM kids, they all said. They have been through so much.

I adored their affection. I idolized it and it soon became like an addiction. I loved receiving pity, I loved their comfort, I loved their condolences. I loved the tag in bolded letters, it gave me a personality and made me important.

I drowned in it. It was painful, but I loved every second.

CHAPTER 10

The days after that I went to a couple other post-graduation parties. They were fun, simple, and I got to see other senior friends before they left. A party of my own was coming up as well, my fifteenth birthday party! I was so excited to see my friends there and enjoy a night with them.

The party went spectacularly, almost everyone I invited came, and it wasn't too intricate. We made it simple so that my friends wouldn't get triggered from flashing lights or loud noises. So, we held it at a recreational center near my house. It was a meaningful night for me, having my friends around and being able to eat and dance with them. They had loads of fun, especially as most of them had never been to a quinceañera before. It felt nice to dress up and have a night about me and my friends.

We had some conflict previously on where we would hold the reception. I previously wanted something extravagant, like a ballroom we could rent out. One night, after weeks of deciding where it should be, my parents decided it would be better if I refrained from making it all about myself. They mentioned a simple and quiet party would be favorable, especially in light of the shooting. I didn't agree. I was frustrated; it was supposed to be the one night that could focus on me. However, after some thinking, I gave in, realizing a smaller place at a smaller price would be better for our family.

Later, it didn't matter as much. I knew that no matter what, as long as I had people who cared for me nearby, it would be a fun night.

It was going seamlessly. People were dancing, eating, and giving me gifts. Other than later on, when a balloon popped and everybody turned their heads in shock. Some of us laughed about it, but I was sort of confused about why I got scared when the balloon popped. I didn't think I had PTSD or any other disorder that would cause me to get triggered. I ignored it for the most part.

After my quinceañera, I opened up the many gifts I got. It was almost pleasant to forget about the incident and enjoy a night with my friends.

The fun was soon over. The next day, our family sat down to talk about Luke's intentions in our house, and some moral disruptions they had while they allowed Luke to live there. It stirred up a lot of disappointment and anger within us at the moment, especially due to the fact that it was brought up a day after the quinceañera. We all sat together in our living room as the tension and anxiety locked my knees up. My parents then began to mention the possibility of removing Luke from our house entirely—the same sibling who was sleeping in the same room as me my entire life, who bought clothes with me, who shared delightful holiday nights with me. I brushed it off—my parents might have been bluffing about it. Yet, I could see their eyes held betrayal and confusion. Luke had already planned to move out due to the tension of the situation, so I deeply wished that he could plan as needed and leave without any turbulence. I was hoping, praying that everything would go smoothly, that Luke could leave with not so much as a whisper. Unfortunately, I had to expect that those prayers would be in vain.

The next few days, my sibling began to pack so he could leave. We were going to a program over the weekend in a week or so—STEM gave out sponsorships for an educational leadership program over the weekend. I got to go for free since I registered early, but my father had to pay extra for Luke as he was late to sign up. We were unsuspecting of anything that would happen next. When I saw the duffle bag on my sibling's bunk, I just hoped it was for the program.

The day that it happened was a fine summer day. I was relaxing and eating out with my father and siblings, as my mom and Jimmy were away overseas. My mother was visiting family and doing business, and Jimmy was visiting his girlfriend at the time. Charlie came along and we had a nice outing—but when we went home, things went a little haywire.

I was relaxing in my mom's room when I heard zipping and rustling next door. I peeked into my room and saw Luke hurriedly gather things into his duffle bag, including art supplies and clothes. I asked what was happening, but it was difficult to pry anything out. He just looked up at me, paused, and then continued to scramble. I decided to call my mom; I had a feeling that something wasn't right. I tried to explain and my mom requested that I hand the phone to Luke. They talked, the both of them. I realized a change in Luke's expression—maybe, just maybe, he was thinking about staying a little while longer. I was garnering hope—but suddenly, I saw my sibling ask "hello" into the phone. Charlie called, interrupting my mom's dialogue. My phone was handed back to me, Luke's expression returned to blank. I felt the hope I previously had sink right into my shoes. I begged him to try and talk to my mother again, but I was brushed off.

I went on the phone with Charlie and told him what happened. I was upset, at him and the situation, but he couldn't have known. He told me he was coming over as soon as he could.

I was in my front yard, hoping to escape the difficult scene that was happening inside the house. Of course, Luke attempted to talk to my father about it. Charlie eventually came, which was fortunate because he was there for me. I was still mad, and I wanted to blame him for interrupting my mom's call with Luke—but I was far too anxious to be angry. I met with the supposed person who would be harboring Luke after the situation was figured out. He parked in front of my house—and he talked to me while waiting. The arguments could be heard from outside. As soon as Luke ran out, they both got in and drove as fast as possible away from us. I wept even more—I didn't know what happened inside the house, but I knew it was bad. I knew I'd never be able to get the same Luke back.

I didn't even want to think about how upset my dad was, having to handle it all alone. Eventually, the police were there. Someone called them, which wasn't great for my trauma—the same police cars and lights, blended with the anxiety coursing through my veins, reminded me of the day the shooting happened. An officer outside stayed with Charlie, David, and I as we waited for an interrogation to be done inside. He asked me if I knew Luke's whereabouts, and I, exasperated, sighed and told him I had no idea. I was never told any details—I was just the first person who knew. The officer tried consoling us by saying adolescents are troublesome, and he had his own that were troublemakers too. It didn't really help, but I appreciated the effort.

We were later asked if we had any contact with Luke. I was evidently blocked on every social media app imaginable, so I tried talking to Luke's partner, and I eventually got in touch. We met on a video call—the room he settled in was dim and daunting. I could see the same duffle bag that he packed earlier in what used to be the room we shared. I said that the police wanted to talk, and that Luke and whoever else was involved should come as soon as possible.

They eventually all made their way back. I ran over to hug Luke—even if I was mad, I still felt love, and I was worried sick. The police then asked us to step aside so they could talk to Luke and his driver. Two officers investigated under a bright yellow street lamp.

After things cooled off, and the investigations were done, they found the situation to be stable. Luke went away, and we had to go back into our now disturbed home. I tried asking an officer if I could stay at Charlie's place, just for the night, but we figured it was easier since the trip to the program over the weekend was in the morning. Plus, my dad didn't need any additional getaways. It was going to be a lot to tough out—from the restless night, to the awkward long car ride in the early morning.

It was upsetting for everyone. I wept a lot that evening. I couldn't grasp the fact that Luke wanted to move on. I felt like he left me behind, and put our relationship at jeopardy for the chance of a better future. I missed our companionship, our nights together, and our relationship. Luke was close to me in a way no one else was. He understood me. I felt betrayed at the moment—I knew now that my roommate and companion was going to be a stranger. It would take a while until I could accept the fact that he needed to move on.

I felt sour in the aftermath of the cataclysmic events. Rage and bitterness entered our home. None of us had yet recovered from what had happened—even our mother, who was overseas, had to lock herself away to cry.

I slowly, heavily marched to my room after packing my things for the program. I was tired. My makeup was running down my face and my hair was in disarray. I was wearing such a stupid outfit—something about hot sauce was on my shirt. The house became dimmer now that Luke was gone. Charlie tried to console me over text. He was there for it all, so he knew how frustrated and exhausted I was. I couldn't bring myself to do anything but lay in my bed, hopeless, afraid. We had a bunk bed in our room. Luke always slept in the bunk above because I was always too scared to be that high up. He was always the braver one, but now, I had no one to rely on when struggling with my loneliness. For the first time in my entire life, I was sleeping alone. I stayed up staring at the wooden planks holding up the mattress. Was Luke thinking the same thing right now, being in a stranger's home? What emotions were there? I blamed Luke for a lot of things then. Previously, it was the shooting that caused all my problems. Now, it was all because of this.

I was half thankful that this happened the night before we had to leave for the program. In a way, I wanted to get away for a bit from everything. I viewed it as an escape rather than a benefit. Yet, I had no idea what I was about to experience. Little did I know, this wasn't just a convenient getaway.

On the drive there, it was silent. We had to awkwardly tag David along, since Luke obviously dipped. It was relieving in a way—I knew Luke would feel uncomfortable in the setting we would be in. The timing couldn't have been better, and I was glad I could be away from my family. Well, not in entirety—David was coming along as a substitute after all. For him, he felt as if he wasn't supposed to be there. He felt like he didn't deserve to experience everything he was about to experience—but he would be proven wrong.

I felt uneasy and anxious entering the program. My mother hadn't gotten back yet from her trip overseas, but she already expressed her devastation from the news. I wanted to be there for my family, and I felt disheartened leaving, but I was glad I had time away in any case.

The days almost flew by. It was an amazing experience. It was powerful and impacting to hear keynote speakers and to be with my team. After only four days, strangers felt like family. I was able to talk about my experience with the shooting, minus the stress of politics or pressure to seem okay. People understood me, and it gave me perspective to know about their lives as well. It gave me comfort to know other people had struggles. Even if it's trivial to assume you're the only one, I still felt alone.

Several students from STEM also came. They were as socially anxious as I was, waiting for someone to talk or approach them first. They would stand around the room with their hands folded, almost frozen as if waiting for a command. Sometimes, I felt that way too. No one understood why I was so distant. I wished they would leave me alone. Yet, if they left me alone, I'd be back to wishing I had someone to talk to. I relied on Charlie many times at the beginning to feel less lonely and pass the time while at the program. I felt stuck—even if I was given all the opportunities to converse with others, I was reserved. Only speak when spoken to, I told myself.

The program was at a college with dorm rooms available for students. It was awesome. We had working showers with hot water, three meals a day, and comfortable beds. It was also a privilege to listen to inspirational speakers and what advice they had to give.

At lunch one day, we sat at black round tables with other speakers. We could converse with them, and the purpose was to receive something from talking to them. I sat with a businesswoman and she asked us what school we went to. Oh, yes, the dreaded question. The question I attempted to avoid for months. I didn't respond, but David did and said he would go next year. She glanced at my lanyard, which held a tag of my school name, gasped, and made sure to give condolences.

I was so annoyed that I had to confront something like that yet again. I only nodded along, and every now and then, I'd mutter a "thanks." I didn't want to experience it again; the condolences, the "your cat died" face, especially as this wasn't an affection I particularly enjoyed at the time. I would've enjoyed it before, but I hoped to get away from all the pity, especially after Luke left. All these unfortunate events made me feel like crawling into a hole to be left alone to wallow forever. She meant well, I knew that, yet I still hoped that the program would be some sort of an escape from everything I experienced so far.

The program was instead something that made me face my struggles, which I am forever grateful for—yet, she seemed so sorry for me. The pity was something I hated from people who thought they understood how I was feeling. The end of the story back then was that they didn't understand. They only wanted to get a story out of me, like the media. When they did, they could tell others that they met a school shooting survivor. It didn't feel like they were considerate of what I felt; all they wanted was the story.

I glanced at her in a deliberate manner between chews of my food. She didn't have my respect any longer as a businesswoman. All I wanted was to be alone now. I convinced myself I didn't need help or sympathy or pity, I only had myself who understood. It didn't help that I still responded in a negative manner every time I spoke about the shooting. I began to shiver, begging myself to calm down on the inside. I was afraid and nervous again. Even breathing didn't help. Thus, my resistant walls were put up yet again.

After lunch, I attempted a quick escape, but she caught me and dragged me into another conversation about school shootings. She said she knew the principal of Columbine High School personally and gave me his contact. I didn't think much of it then. I stored away his card and brushed off the brief interruption of my peace.

Other people rarely asked about the school on my name tag, unlike her, which I was grateful for.

Later in the day, I saw in the planner that we had to visit Columbine High School. It terrified me. The survivors of Columbine had gone through something way worse than I had. I didn't have a concrete belief that pain is pain, as I do currently. I asked around several times about going to Columbine, even asking if it was necessary. I decided to just live in the moment and worry about visiting Columbine when the time came—it was a few days away anyhow.

The day after that, I forgot all about it, as I was having such a good time at the program. I was experiencing community, laughter, and real joy spread through connection. I had the opportunity to listen to more great inspirational speakers. They gave me new perspectives on situations I've had in my life.

One of the speakers mentioned that we had no idea what we were about to experience. I became cynical at hearing this, but he was right. I could guess all I wanted, but the truth was that I wasn't prepared for what was about to happen.

CHAPTER 11

The day came where we were about to visit Columbine.

I dressed up and got ready, a little nervous, not anxious or scared, but sort of apathetic. Yet, I was willing to listen and experience.

We arrived at the school, and it was like walking on an unknown surface, as if we stepped upon another eerie realm. Policemen were circulating the school and checking the perimeter. I looked around as we got inside, and I felt shocked by the beauty of the school. It was just a normal school that forever had a tainted name, like STEM. Students walked through the same halls before they gossiped and planned to hang out later after their history class.

I felt uneasy in the gymnasium where we ended up for the first half. We were playing competitive games in teams, restricted from the presence of our cell phones. Yet, I couldn't resist, I felt as if something was happening. I discreetly grabbed my phone from where we placed our belongings and made my way to the restroom. To my disappointment, I was correct.

I found a few articles describing, in full, the plans of Devon and Alec. I snuck away to a stall to read it in silence.

I had the previous notion that Devon led Alec into the crime, but it was Alec, in actuality, who threatened Devon and took the role of ringleader. To add, Alec wanted to kill himself before the police caught him, but they tackled him at the right time. Devon also attempted to tell someone before it all happened, but didn't due to Alec's death threats. I couldn't believe it at all. Alec had always been a close friend of mine. I kept thinking that I should have told a counselor the minute I saw Alec being suspicious.

I couldn't have known. No one could have.

I tried to go back with normality, as if I didn't read anything, and the day went on. It became difficult to keep a smile and maintain the air of playfulness. Usually, I enjoy competition, but the news I received dragged my mind down and prevented me from enjoying myself.

Afterward, we all shuffled into the auditorium. The seats were teal-gray colored, and rigidly textured, like carpet. We had the wonderful opportunity of listening to the past principal of Columbine. He was a middle-aged man with a hearty smile. His appearance was one accentuated by age, but he seemed like a man you could converse with at ease. The businesswoman a few days ago mentioned his name to me, but I never minded it. It felt like she was pitying me yet again, hoping I'd find a connection with the man. It wasn't on my checklist to greet him. I knew he'd been through many things. I'd assume that as a principal, you have high hopes for your students; you treat them as *family*. It must be a terrible feeling to know one of your own had evil thoughts and desires like that.

Even if his story was humbling and touching, I got anxious as he spoke. I began to tremble again as he talked about his experience at Columbine on April 20, 1999. His friend sacrificed himself as the shooter was pointing the gun at him. He had to lead a handful of girls from a locker room to the gymnasium while the shooter was still roaming the hallways. Not to mention his need to keep brave after his friend jumped in front of the shooter.

I still felt numb. My peers had tearful eyes and gave a standing ovation. I followed, not exactly tearing up, but giving the man the applause that he deserved. I just couldn't bring myself to cry. Deep down I felt I couldn't—I had to remain strong. It was so obvious that I would cry at something like that. I was over ambitious, trying to subvert their expectations. This was building up; I felt it trying to release from inside me. It wasn't pleasant. It felt like an intense need to scream, but repressing it to refrain from scaring anyone.

They instructed us to follow others to the memorial nearby. I stayed behind, walking to the stage and shifting toward the principal. I waited in a line, avoiding eye contact with him until it was my turn to speak.

He turned to me with kind eyes and a smile on his face. Suddenly, I found it hard to speak. I got choked up, my fingers froze—and even if I didn't want to cry, I felt my eyes watering. I greeted him, mentioning I was from STEM. I spoke in an almost superficial manner about how his speech touched me. If I spoke the truth from my heart, I would've made a fool of myself crying. His eyes held so much depth, it was extremely difficult to bottle it in. We talked for a few moments, and then I went to follow the last few people on their way to the memorial. I walked alone.

It was windy, the chill biting at my nose and cheeks as I made my way to the memorial alone. It was quiet, peaceful almost, but the air around me was eerie and cold. I got lost on my way and began to wander on a field near a park, aimless in my direction. There was a skatepark that the principal mentioned in his speech, a gazebo, and a large grassy field. A few families with toddlers walked down from what seemed like a festival of some sort on the top of a hill. It seemed like a grim day to hold a festival. I saw kids with face paint and balloons and candy. It felt wrong to me when compared to the heaviness I felt in my heart. The pop of colors from the festival contrasted from the clouds and the arid chill.

I found a team leader walking with someone else from the program. I asked him to take me to the memorial since I lost my way. He led me there, and we laughed a little at the irony of the festival.

I now saw the memorial from the top of the hill. I saw David and other familiar faces from the program spotted about the stone layout. They paced around the memorial carrying dejected mannerisms and expressions. They swallowed tears every now and then, their eyes tracing the words carved into the stone.

Everyone had their arms crossed over their stomachs. It was as if they were trying to protect themselves from the biting cold in summer. My old peers from STEM were glancing around the memorial, frozen, unsure where to start, or even how to start. The air was nipping at my skin, and it didn't help that I was already shivering from anxiety. I took a deep breath and pushed down any fears or cautions I had.

My team leader told me where to start. There was a stone wall curling around the memorial in a protective manner. Decked upon it were black slabs engraved with the quotes of the Columbine community—parents, students, teachers, and families.

I read the words rather fast. I didn't want to analyze any more than I had to. It would make me cry on the spot, and I wanted to seem resilient, especially in that moment.

Something rather uncanny stood out to me—every phrase engraved on the slabs gave me a strange feeling of déjà vu. I've heard it before. Words said by the Columbine community reminded me of things said by the STEM community.

I moved on to look at the fountains, averting my gaze from the text for a moment. I didn't need to cry. I wasn't supposed to cry. I needed to be there for others, for David.

I took a deep breath before facing the memorial stones of the thirteen in the center. They were all there, the casualties of the Columbine massacre. Added to the names below were pieces of sentimental information—a description, a note, perhaps a diary entry— anything reminiscent of who they were and how others saw them lay engraved below their names.

There were groups surrounding the black engraved stones, so I had to wait my turn to view them.

When it was my turn, my expression turned pensive. I read each one with some sort of ironic smile. I kept imagining my name on the stones, my songs and diary entries below my name. I imagined others reading my memorial. They would be pitying the abrupt death I experienced. They would think of the dreams stripped away from me, all because someone hateful had a gun. They would be wondering why they lived in such a world, a world of hate.

I came across a written diary entry from one of the thirteen. It was beautiful. A young lady wrote that she dreamt of sitting with Jesus in a beautiful flower field. My eyes watered. It only made me wonder how the most faithful and loving people had to leave.

My heart felt exhausted after reading the few others, including Rachel's stone. I pondered how different the world would be if they had a real chance at life.

CHAPTER 12

I saw David sit on a bench-like structure made out of the rocks that surrounded and made up the memorial. I wanted to approach him, but he seemed lost in thought. He was looking up at the cloudy sky, pursing his lips in wonder. He then glanced around the memorial before standing and walking away.

He left. I went to sit in his place. I gazed at the ground with a blank stare.

I always swallowed my tears before. I always wanted to seem like the brave one—the survivor. But only this once, I thought, all these months, all this time, was I there for myself? Or only for others? What was this all for? Why?

As I stared down at the ground, my eyes welled with tears. But I didn't swallow them or stop them. They fell on my cheek and I let them.

I began sobbing and clutching at my sides. I felt sick. I felt like there was a chance I could've been on a memorial. I could've been one of the casualties. A pitiful death it would've been—not an honorable one like Kendrick's. A death as a result from my cowardice and stupidity. A death in vain.

A couple of classmates from STEM came immediately to comfort me and hug me. But I kept repeating under my breath, "it could've been me, it could've been me."

I finally felt understood.

My peers, who I hardly even looked at when I was a student at STEM, were stroking my back and making sure I felt alright. I couldn't stop crying. It was like an emotional dam had opened up inside of me. I blocked off all my emotions for the good of others, for the good of my family, and for the good of my peers. Now they manifested in my tears and my choked sobs.

After a few minutes, I felt okay. It felt like the burden finally lifted off my shoulders. Finally, I cried to someone. I thanked my peers, who were survivors like me, and we rose to see the rest of the memorial.

We climbed a hill and at the top was the most beautiful view of the mountains. I sat at a bench, feeling the chill on my forearms and my face, and I felt thankful for the chill. I wished that Kendrick could've seen the view. There was a beautiful lake with mist over the mountains, and trees surrounding the lake.

I overheard two girls behind me complain of the cold and I became bitter. It felt to me as if they were completely ignorant of what we experienced only minutes ago. I got up after they left, along with my STEM peers who stuck by me.

We began walking back to the school, where we would have dinner. We were solemn and quiet. As we walked down the hill, we saw a boy do a flip trick over the border between the grassy hill and the ground of the memorial. We all scoffed and shook our heads, yet I wanted more. I wanted to shout at him. I wanted to make him feel ashamed for his blatant disregard of respect for us and for the memorial.

But I didn't, I knew it would be better if I kept in my anger.

As we walked in the parking lot, and onto the pavement, I saw small, green plants creep out of the cracks in the ground. It inspired me.

If those plants could grow through the cracks, through a place of no light and be able to find the light, I could too. I could find the growth in the cracks and find a way out of my sadness. Even in the bitter and tense cold, they find a way to thrive, regardless of the lack of sun.

Dinner was waiting inside the cafeteria of the school. I got my plate and went to sit with the usual group. I formed a friend group of sorts at the program, as I like having people to stick to. I usually depended on this group to have a seat whenever we ate. I sat with them for lunch the previous hours before, but they moved to the table adjacent. The seats at the table were all taken, and their uncomfortable glances gave me the message. My friend from STEM took note of this, that it was strange, but we sat at another table and ate our food, giving it no more thought.

I wanted to speak of how I felt, but I knew it would make it awkward. I had already cried on my peer's shoulder, and I didn't want to bother him any longer. He really wasn't that type of person, nor were we close. I finished my dinner quickly, but still felt excluded by my usual group. It felt as if they didn't want to touch the sensitive girl. They had no intention to face deep emotions. It seemed as though they wanted to give us space and respect how we felt, which I understood, but I felt hurt. I would have felt better if someone other than a STEM kid confronted me. I wish they told me they understood and that they were there for me. Those were my emotions at the moment.

I went to ask my team leader if I could vent. I told him everything I had been feeling for the past few months along with what I felt at the memorial.

He understood me and listened to my ramblings. I held him back from getting dinner, but he was happy I talked to him. Talking with him gave me inspiration to speak later on to my peers at the program.

I had the courage to stand and tell everyone my experience at the memorial. I was no longer angry—-I felt changed. I began crying again, and my friend came up to me and embraced me as I spoke.

I spoke of how I felt about imagining myself in the memorial. I spoke of the growth I saw through the cracks. I even mentioned the rude teenager who jumped over the separation.

And afterward, I got appreciation, tears, compliments, and I never felt more loved. I felt like people listened to me, finally—after all these months of pushing down what I felt to listen to others. I figured out I needed to heal myself first. I finally met acceptance with the events I went through. I accepted and validated my emotions, my tears, my anger, my sorrow, everything.

It was the first time I felt that way about my trauma. Trauma— yes, I had it, and it was valid, as valid as my peers who were nearer to the gunshots.

I found real acceptance and joy at the program. I can never thank them enough for that.

CHAPTER 13

Ileft the program sorrowful; I had so much to thank everyone for, but I had to leave. I made some amazing friendships there, and I felt accepted for the first time in months.

There was this one part of the program that I will never forget. It was the last day, and we shared our personal life with our team members. They instructed us to close our eyes and wrap our arms around each other as they played soft music in the back. It almost felt orchestrated only for that specific moment. Instant joy instilled in my heart, and a sheepish smile grew on my face—but most likely because I thought it was stupid at first.

They told us to imagine ourselves in this huge field of flowers. I saw myself standing in the middle, breathing in the soothing scent of dusk. I watched the sun descend behind the mountains and offer me its last bit of golden warmth on my face. Beige plants surrounded me—feather reed grass, stalks that were similar-looking to wheat. The wind blew them with a gentle breeze.

We were then supposed to imagine our troubles behind us as we turned around. I turned around and I saw my trauma. I saw my past, my upbringing, my enemies, my struggles, everyone who had denied me before. At first, I wondered why it didn't seem like a dark cloud rushing toward me. Though, as I paused and studied everything, it didn't seem like something from a deranged horror film. It seemed dull and tired compared to my golden surroundings. It didn't haunt me; it was all there, stagnant, a part of me, yet it never chased after me. It was all there, seeming to smile at me and encourage me.

I acknowledged this and imagined myself turning forward once more with tears forming in my eyes.

We had to imagine something different now. As they described it to me, I saw my family appear at first. I saw my siblings, my parents, and everyone else who encouraged me and supported me first. Then I saw my friends, Hannah and Mandy alongside them, standing next to Charlie. Then, a whole string of familiar faces came up behind them. My friends from STEM, the friends I made in the program—my dogs, even. They were all cheering for me, inviting me to come toward them, and I saw that this was my purpose. Not only my purpose, but my *future*. Their faces looked warm and inviting. The sun glowed down and shadowed their faces from the other side. They looked real, vibrant, *there*.

I began to run toward them and the music escalated. They cheered and cheered and called my name and I ran faster, never looking back. As I got closer, I saw tears of joy welling in their eyes and falling on their cheeks with grace. Finally, I reached their embrace. I was home.

I pressed my cheek into their shoulders and wept just like I wept into Charlie's shoulders on the day of the shooting. They all told me that they loved me. I wept not only in this daydream but also on the outside too. My friends gripped at my sides and cried like babies as well. The experience was strange. It felt as though all of us reached acceptance at the same time. Everyone, from the tall jocks to the quiet kids of the group, choked on their sobs.

The program not only helped me accept my trauma a little more but also helped me find what happiness meant.

I was more mindful. I was mindful of the time I spent looking at my phone, mindful of my family, and more accepting of the trauma of others. I kept comparing in the past, as if I could compare the pain we felt. I compared what I experienced to other experiences all the time.

I kept in mind what I thought about the growth through the cracks in the asphalt, and I have grown a lot since then. I'm starting school again and helping others with what they feel. I've loved Luke through everything, and feel the same with the rest of the family.

It's still tough sometimes. I see the things that happen, the El Paso shooting and others, I hear about them in the news and I get angry. I get angry because it's as if nothing has changed since STEM. I get angry because the generalizations the media makes are the same ones from our time. It's unfortunate I can't change things this instant and make it better for the survivors of shootings.

Yet, healing takes time, as does change within the world. I hope this book—my words, my emotions, my tears, my *experience*—can cause a shift in people's hearts.

This is my experience—and it's ongoing, the healing never stops. My attachment to STEM will be eternal. I will always think of STEM when incidents like this happen. I will remember the community that formed and the healing that took place within our hearts. I've found acceptance, but the healing will continue. The only thing that stops me from healing is the choice I have to not heal.

Alec McKinney received the sentence of life in prison without parole. The moment I heard the news, I felt resentful. I felt angered by the fact that he was crying in front of the witnesses in court, wanting pity. He wasn't upset for the cruelties he committed; he was upset he got caught. I justified the response of Kendrick's parents. The pain a parent feels when they lose a child is inexplicable, and they had every right to tell Alec to go to hell. I'm not ready to forgive yet, even if it's been years. It's an ongoing process and something I can never forget. Someday, I'll have the strength to forgive.

In instances like these, people have a choice to accept their trauma or to deny it. Many times, I've denied my trauma, but I still had the choice to start the harrowing journey of healing.

The mindset is most important. You can drag your feet, complain, whine, and be stuck in the stunt mindset, or, you can be willing to feel, to walk toward happiness with a growth mindset. I didn't choose the latter the first time. I dragged my feet on the path and complained. I thought I could heal by thinking not of myself first, but others. Then, I turned around. I took a step back and wondered if I was doing the right thing.

I didn't and still don't think I did something wrong by having the wrong mindset. It was all a part of my journey, of what I needed to accept myself and my trauma.

I still struggle. Healing isn't linear; I have good days and bad days. Sometimes, I get scared when I see police cars collecting outside of a building. Many times, I feel intensely anxious in public spaces. I don't want anyone to think I'm perfect and healed now. I still shiver when I speak of what happened.

I felt different when speaking to others of my experience. I felt out of place and I still do sometimes. I'm not like my friends who were near the gunshots. Some people view my experience as a lucky chance—if I hadn't been away doing the project during that hour, I would be across the hall from the room where it happened.

I got lucky in some perspectives—but to me, I lucked out. Sometimes, I have this feeling of being stuck and lost, as if I'm going nowhere, and I'm back to square one. I have yet to accept this will affect me forever. I know I'll always feel unsafe when I'm in public. I'll always feel inferior to my peers who chose the preppy high schools when I insisted on going to STEM.

The truth is that I'll always feel scared. In the program, they mentioned that fear is a liar. It's something that brings us down. I, for one, feel like I can't be at peace like some of my classmates from my old school. It's easy to feel like that when you happen to meet by coincidence at a coffee shop or see their photos on social media. They look happy, and all you can remember is that you should've chosen something else. Then, none of it would have happened.

Yet, if I never went to STEM, I never would have met Charlie. I would never experience the joy of singing with him. Better yet, I would've never experienced a fulfilling love later. I would've never had the chance to perform in the way I wanted to. I would've never met the people who helped me grow.

I often ask myself, if I had the chance to go back, would I do it in a different way? Would I choose another preppy high school? Would I change things if I could?

They're tricky questions—but when you deal with something like this, you realize that it's better not to dwell on the "what ifs." I still love many people from STEM and feel like I had an intense change of heart and mind when I attended the school.

It's sad knowing I was close to Alec. Sometimes, it doesn't feel real, that I knew a school shooter, and how he was even so popular at STEM in the first place. I dwell on the question of why, especially why it happened to me rather than any other school. So then, is this the burden I carry on my shoulders? Is this the event that defines me and my future? Of course not—who knows the struggles I will encounter in the future? Perhaps it will affect me more than the events of that summer did.

In retrospection, I look back on the connections I had from STEM that slowly melted away. I walk downtown and see small bands playing live, and remember how I performed with others in small bands or talent shows. I remember the laughs I had sitting in the cafeteria, seeing my friend trying to cut open a hard kiwi with a plastic spoon. I look back at the trivial delicacy of school lunch, the comfort in the consistency of half-baked mozzarella sticks. We would look in scorn at the endless assignments, claiming we hated our teachers, but come back every day, looking forward to the mindless banter we would have before class started. I miss it, pretending to look at a computer screen to hide away, but chuckle softly at the stupid jokes the jocks made in English class.

I like to think that my peers at STEM felt the same—but it's crushing to even imagine the heartbreak after never being able to see your home classroom in the same light. The room that never used the artificial overhead lights, but instead relied on the dim glow of a computer screen projected. It was the last class of the day for those in Ms. Harper's room. They were relying on seeing their friends in the cafeteria lounge upstairs right after. They were feeling that same excitement watching the time tick down. Everyday walking into that class was muscle memory. Most of them didn't even feel the need to speculate where to hide if, by chance, a shooter came in that day—until after it happened.

So this is a commemoration. Maybe a blind or naïve one, but a commemoration nonetheless. I commemorate all the innocent souls in that room that fateful day, who didn't even imagine the possibility of something so unimaginable happening in our friendly local town. I commemorate the bravery it took for everyone in that school to escape through the back door or hide behind a weak wooden desk. I commemorate the children who held scissors or an opened marker in their hand, hoping maybe it would protect them against a firearm. I commemorate those who held Kendrick during his last breaths, even if they knew staying there was a risk, because protecting each other meant more than anything. We were called Spartans for a reason.

After May 7th, I would count every single magpie I saw and wonder what all the singles meant. I saw a single one almost every day, and strangely enough, the magpies would be closer every time.

On a chilly and bright January morning, I walked to a nearby coffee shop with David. I felt strangely happy that day.

I saw a single magpie perched on a stone separation as we entered the local shopping center. We were only a couple of feet away from the magpie, and it didn't even flinch as we walked by. I gasped and told David how close we were to the bird. He didn't say much about the matter. He probably thought I was being hooky-dooks again. I felt saddened that my fate was sorrowful, but still admired the beauty of the magpie's feathers.

Then, out of nowhere, a second magpie swooped next to me, perching above the first. And for the first time in forever, there were two. A small smile crept on my lips. *Joy!*